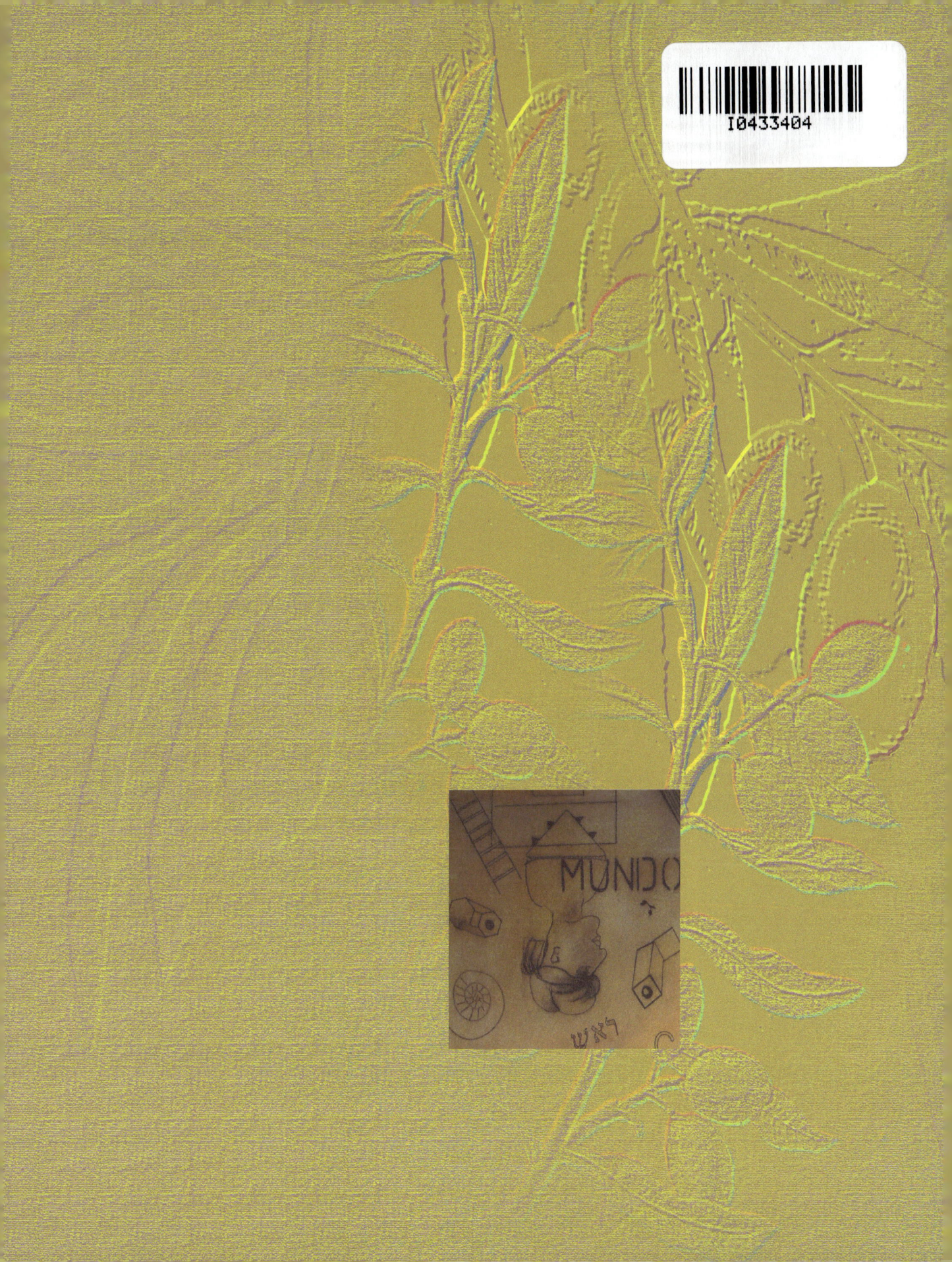

OTHER BOOKS BY GLORIA ABELLA BALLEN
ALL ARE BEST BOOK AWARD WINNERS

THE POWER OF THE HEBREW ALPHABET

NEW WORLD HAGGADAH with Ilan Stavans

GARDEN OF EDEN: PLANTS OF THE HEBREW BIBLE

Creativity and Inspiration

Gloria Abella Ballen

Creativity and Inspiration

Gaon Books

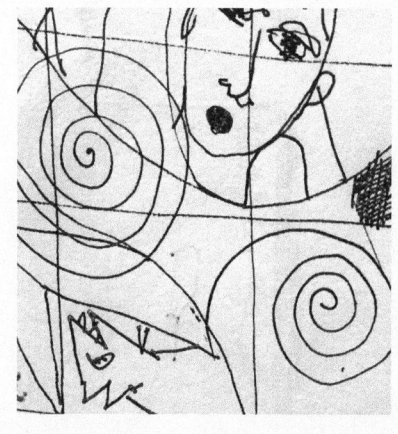

Creativity

*W*here and how do I get the idea for a specific work? I do not know exactly. I start working and a dialogue begins between me and that which is appearing in the piece.

I work every day in the silence of my studio in the company of the plants and birds I see and hear through my windows. In a workshop I did with John Cage in San Juan, Puerto Rico he said, "Silence is the sound of life." I have found his statement to be so true.

For this book I have taken pages from my sketchbooks from different times and places that show some of the sources of inspiration that have fed my silence in the studio and contributed to my art making.

*M*y world is a world in translation
or interpretation through visual paths.

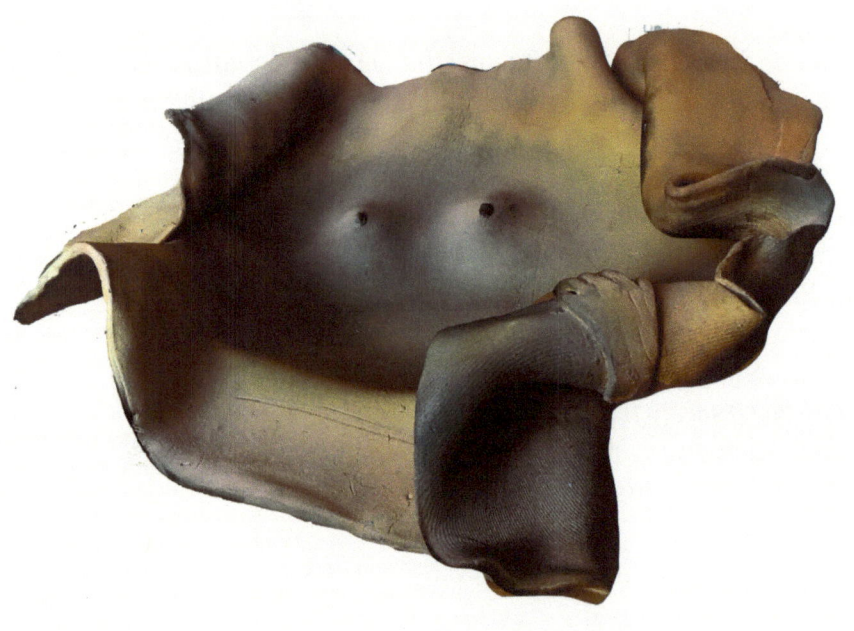

"Ophelia" Inspired by Shakespeare.
Stoneware, stains, smoke

Inspiration

How do I get ideas that result in art? What do we call art? How does art communicate and to whom does it communicate? These are questions that are always posed to artists.

As artists we are members of a particular group influenced by the environments we inhabit whether they be physical, social, cultural, psychological, or artistic, and this becomes the source of our artistic interests and visual responses.

The imaginative and intellectual work I do in the studio is a form of research, an exploration of a particular subject to be developed in a personal visual manner. The development of visual expression, when using the imagination, often draws from memory, which is tinged by feelings. We remember differently each time we access a particular memory or thought of an object or an experience. Memory and remembering are like falling leaves that drift and turn in the air on their downward journey from the tree to its shadow below.

Time is also of consequence. How long ago we experienced the object or the scene affects how detailed it is in our memory and how we render it visually. Here creativity fuses with interpretation, shaping our aesthetic response.

For me, ideas and thoughts often surge from the unconscious, memories or dreams, and I express them visually in drawing or painting, in jewelry and *objets d'art*, or in book images like those in *The Power of the Hebrew Alphabet*, which were based on a dream that letters were coming out of my head and increasing in size as they floated off into space. In that book I approached the meaning of the letters within Jewish kabbalist philosophy, as means of inspiration in order to connect the art with the mystical.

Matisse, the great artist and innovator, said that art should present an illusion of reality. His experimentation and breaking of rules gave way for a new interpretation and definition of space, proportion, color and reality, which together with Picasso in the twentieth century, changed the course of centuries of painting and sculpture giving way to freedom from academicism and leading to new developments in the visual arts.

Individuality of vision for me is what is interesting in an art piece. The challenge of the ambiguous and different pushes our cognitive expectations and adds excitement to find new meanings in what we know as normative.

Although technical knowledge is important to construct an image or deconstruct an idea, technical proficiency is not necessarily the definition of a creative piece. It needs the individual vision to push what we know to new meanings or ways of seeing that would remain in our mind to tickle our perception and expand our imagination.

How much can one consciously absorb from experiences at the time we are living them? It seems as if all we experience goes in our brain, and it comes out later in ways we do not expect and with the transformations that time and new knowledge add to the creative expression.

Working across disciplines and media, from images on paper, painting on canvas, ceramic sculpture, jewelry, and creating books has allowed me to express my vision of the world in aesthetic and metaphysical ways, a specially rich and exciting space.

Color is a beautiful part of our sensuous world, both mysterious and profound. It gives us atmospheric feelings of happiness or quietness, and it alters our mood, as music does. I fly across colors and shapes and juxtapose and deconstruct them in order to put the pieces together in an ambiguous manner to allow the possibility of new meanings that challenge expectations about the known.

As Jacques Derrida, the French philosopher of deconstruction, talks about subjectivity and the debunking of established traditional thought, I too rely on my subjectivity and ambiguity as a way to express my individual ideas about doing art. My works are composed of fragments that wrap around ideas; they are stylised figures sometimes floating in space with unexpected, contradictory and even ambiguous color and placement. Letters and numbers drift as visual elements, often making reference to Jewish mysticism.

My life has been fragmented by living in different parts of the world, experiencing different languages, cultures and mindsets, enfusing my imagination with magic and the flexibility to break old rules and make art in new ways that unconsciously juxtaposes bits and pieces from those lived experiences.

I draw from my experiencing the magnificent colors of the tropics and the richness of Andean vegetation (where I grew up), pre-Columbian gold, textiles and ceramic creations, the expansiveness of the Caribbean Sea with the liquidity of its color, the beauty of Moroccan architecture and art, the lusciousness of an oasis in a Chinese desert, the glow of the desert in Israel, and the infinite open skies of the desert in the American Southwest, which offers me every day happiness. Philosophy, mystical Jewish thought, art history, poetry and music also feed my imagination and art making.

The beauty and richness of Spanish Jewish medieval illuminated manuscripts with their use of gold and silverleaf and warm Mediterranean color have been a source of inspiration for me. In these manuscripts we see the expression of poetry shaped concretely as leaves, flowers, animals or geometric shapes done in tiny letters (micrography) as a manner of adornment and as part of the text itself.

Letters in contemporary expression have given way to a whole field of "visual poetry" where their placement and size become the art itself, going beyond the written text. The letters are the visual poem.

I use randomly placed letters or numbers in my work, and these letters or words dance within the visual field and interact with the images in the total composition, compelling the viewer to find connections that internally relate to the meaning of the piece, and that are suggested through form, shape and the arrangement of the elements. When working with silver I use them as graphic textural elements carved into the surface.

An art piece can be poetic as it elicits feelings from its quietness, from the arrangement of its elements, or from its color.

Working constantly on my own ideas I have developed an individual path that is distinguishable from everyone else. It takes a lot of energy to be creative, and you do what you can do and try to do what you cannot to see the result. Experimentation is a tool that drives creativity.

Knowledge, passion, research, experimentation, observation, listening, and silence are all important elements for inspiration in making art. Doing art constantly is the muse that inspires because one idea brings another with its rainbow of ramifications.

I generally combine disparate elements and sizes and juxtapose different forms in a fragmentary spontaneous manner. I embrace the absurd or the unexpected. Walter Benjamin used his fragmentary style to write about life in Paris through a massive collection of notes written not in a straight cohesive line but more as a lot of thoughts, a jumbled whole, that left ample space for interpretation.

My sketchbooks are non-linear thoughts whether in words or drawings or photos of my paintings and *objects d'art*. They are a repository of some of what has been in my mind, and that influences the art I make. I doodle on a blank page and the lines develop into thoughts that become images which bring new ideas to tickle my imagination to produce new works.

We all are about stories.
The ones we learn and the ones we make
with the tools we have in our vocabulary and imagination.

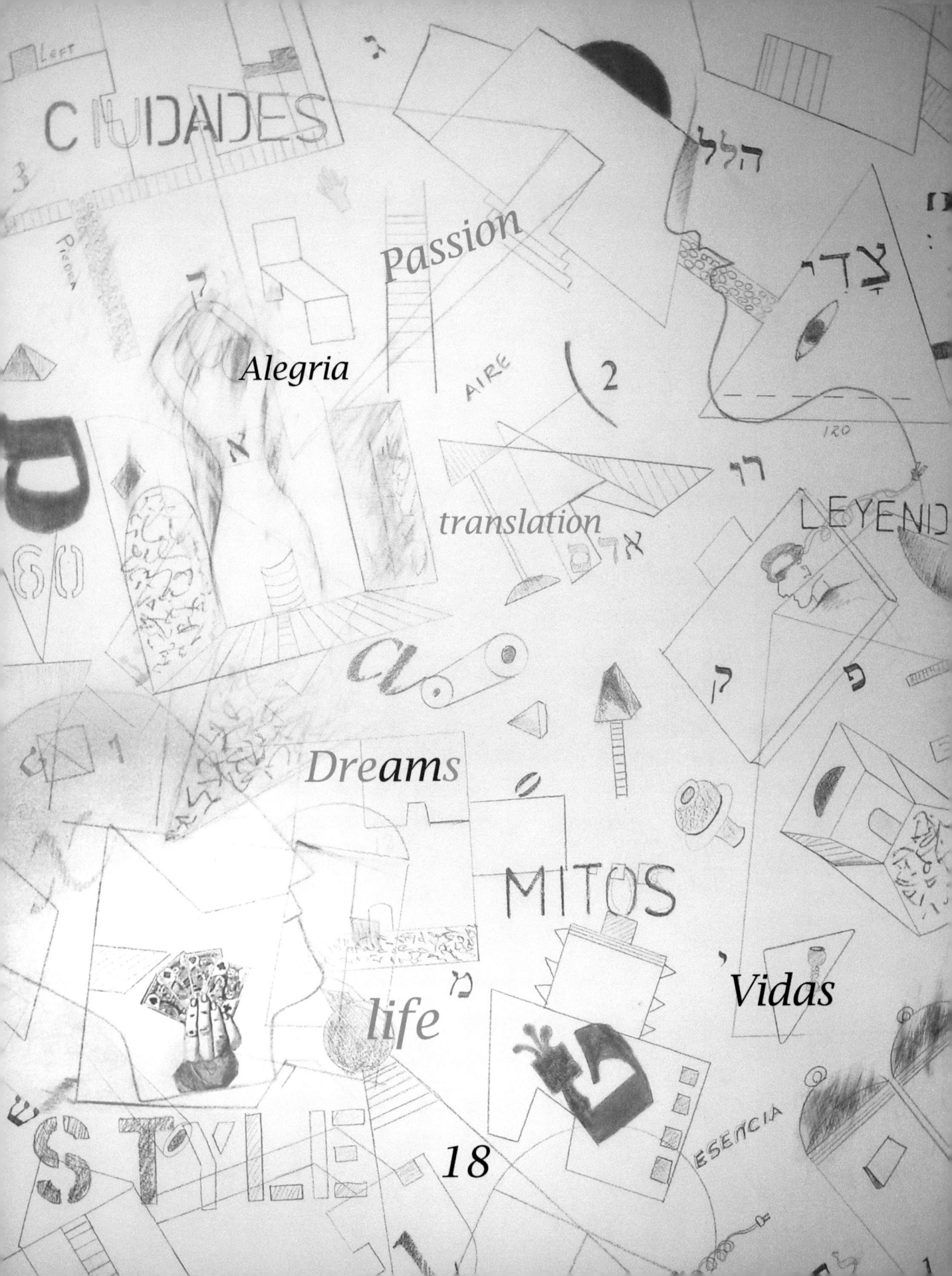

*The following
are
pages from my
sketchbooks,
some of
which I
have carried
through years
of traversing
continents
while
teaching,
doing art
and living.*

Inspiration, observation, doodling, drawing, fragmentation and linguistic and cultural translation have been my constant companions in exploring ideas within a variety of media.

tantos vidas, tantas solitudes
tanto amor —

Vivir, hacer, ser feliz

the research,
the solitude that goes
into a part.
— *Bob Hoskins, actor*

To be alive is to use all your senses to appreciate and enjoy what you see, what you read, what you hear —
Life and Living is a process and it's better when we become aware of things around us!

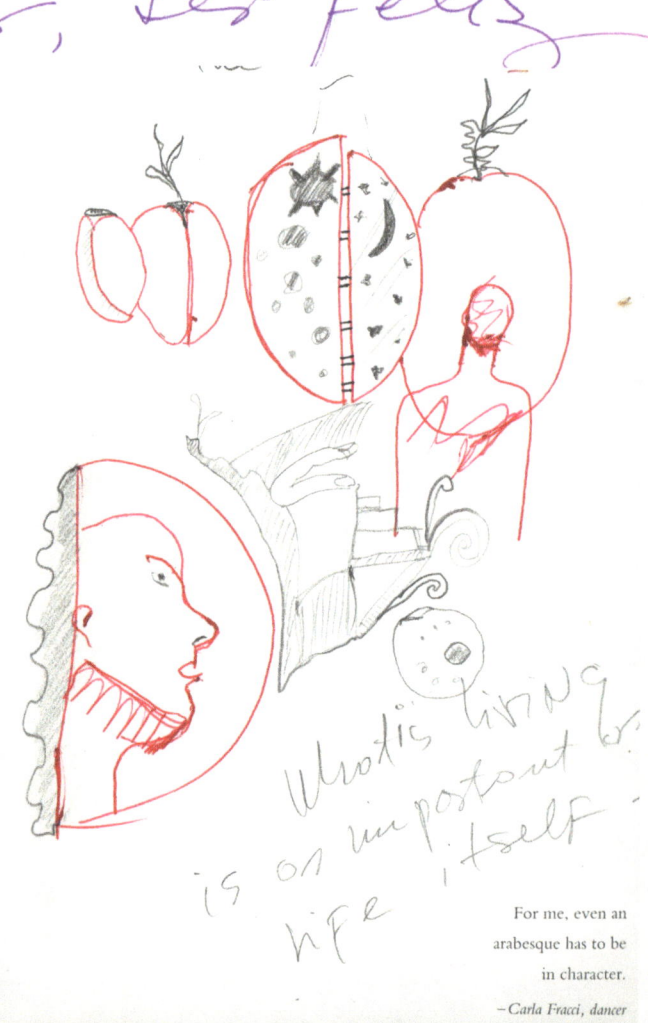

What is living? Living is an important life itself.

For me, even an arabesque has to be in character.
— *Carla Fracci, dancer*

So many lives, so many solitudes
So much love
To live, to do, to be happy
That is an art!
To search and to find is to become happy.
Life is art if you know how to live it.
One has to learn and that is the secret of creating.
To see, to listen, to digest and to do.

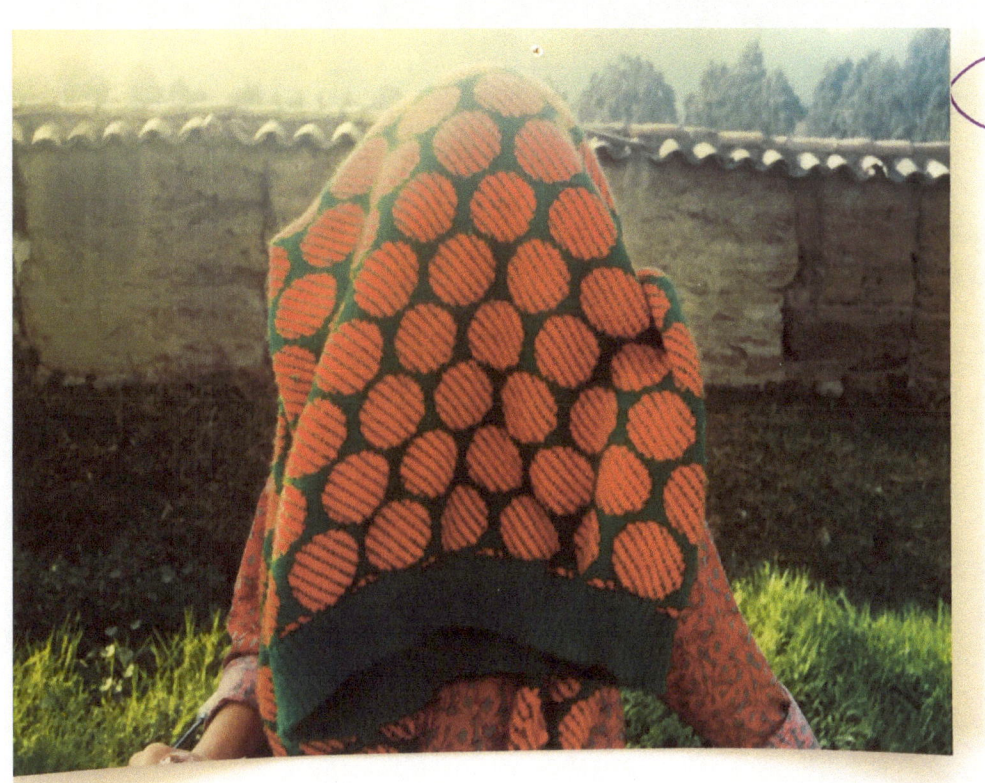

Self portrait

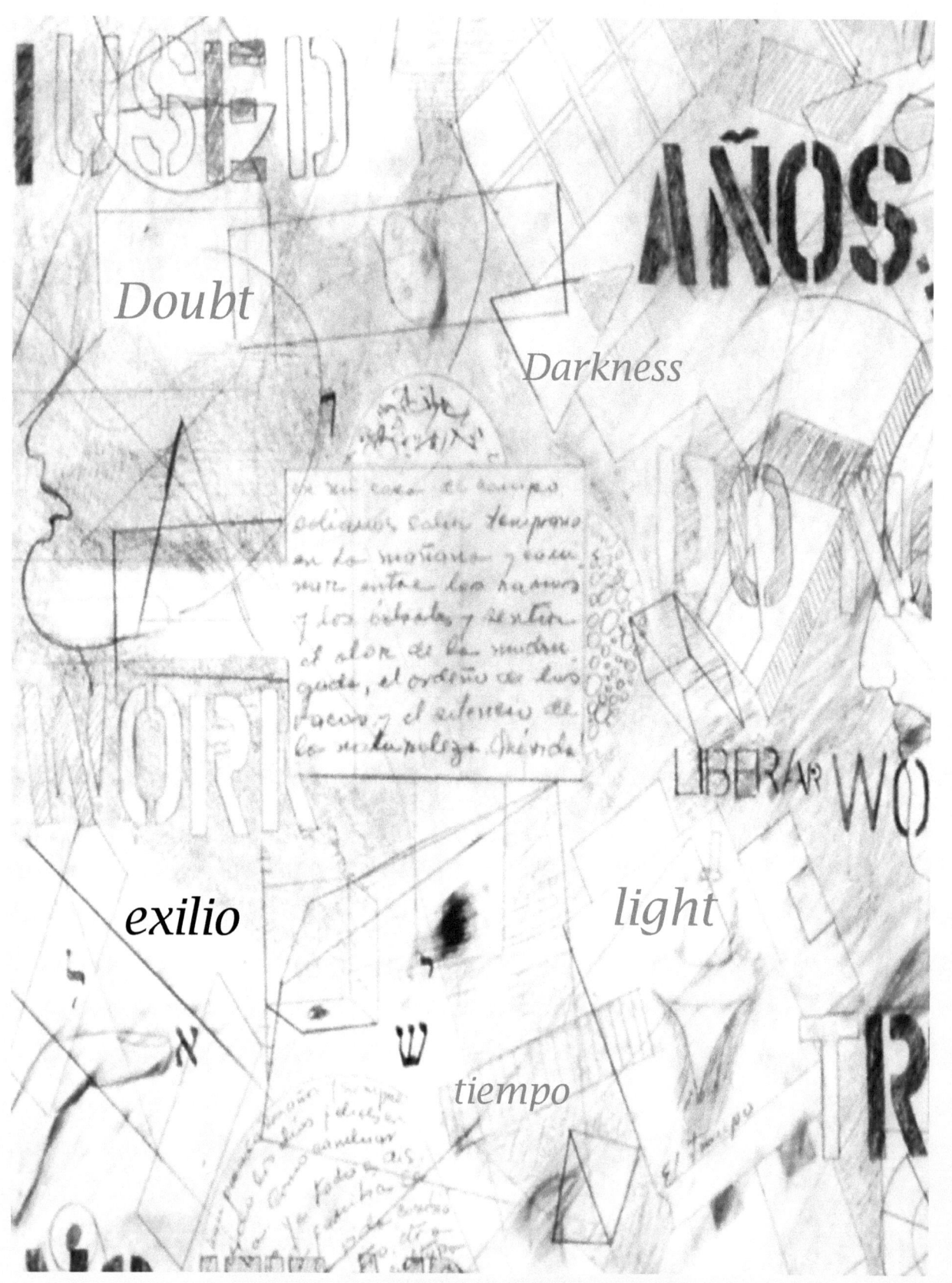

Every time I talk I get the same question. Where are you from? — I don't know anymore — from many places.

Migration, exile, loss and opportunity are part of my identity.

It's like darkess + light put together.

Violence and war in the country made my family scatter

Suddenly I felt alone and dissoriented. But emotionally my family held tightly onto each other and we started again building a new version of the rich creative lines we used to have.

Letting my imagination go and thinking about relationships I just wondered if one could only design one's partner. A photo of a big painting I did in a humorous manner and titled it "Design your partner". Piece by piece as a combination of nature, pieces of colors and letters, more as a ~~sket~~ sewing project.

you do what you can do
and try what you cannot
do to see the results.
Life is trial and error
to find what works.
Everything we do has a
consequence

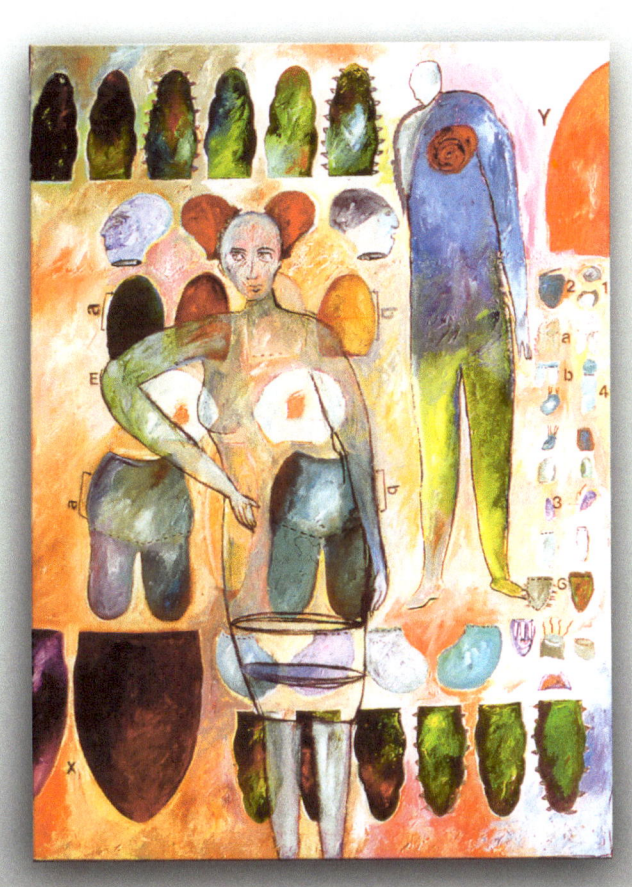

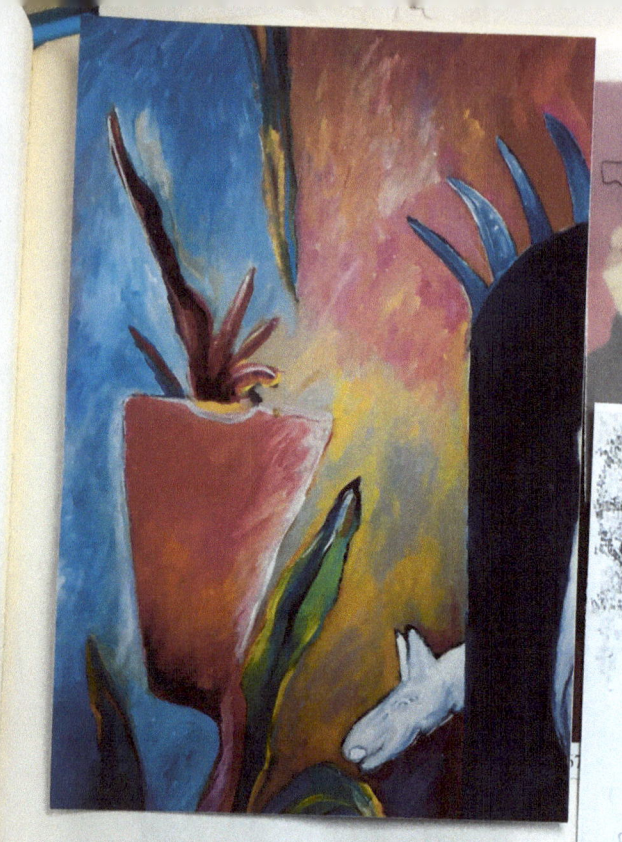
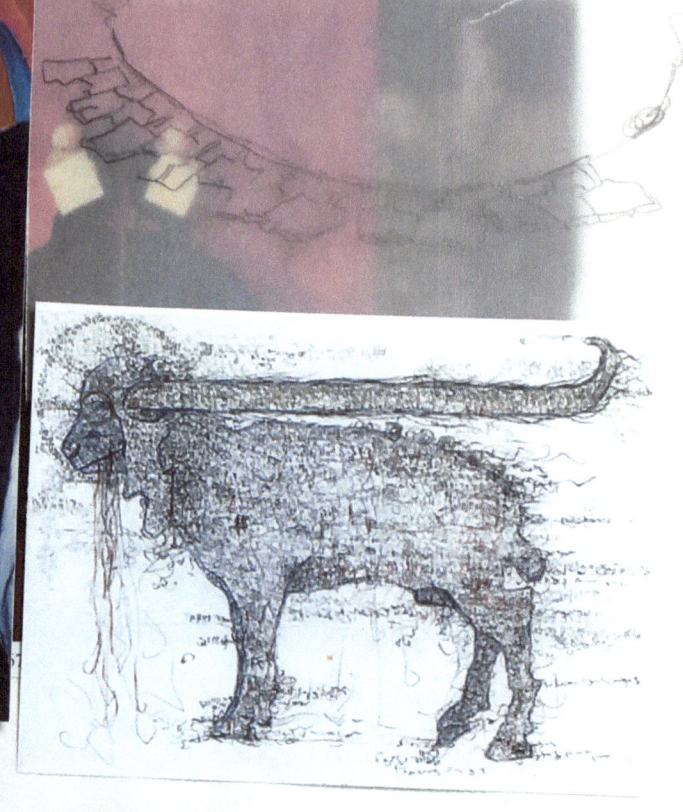

Larry Rivers woo doing research on Eastern European Jews to make his big painting on Russian revolution

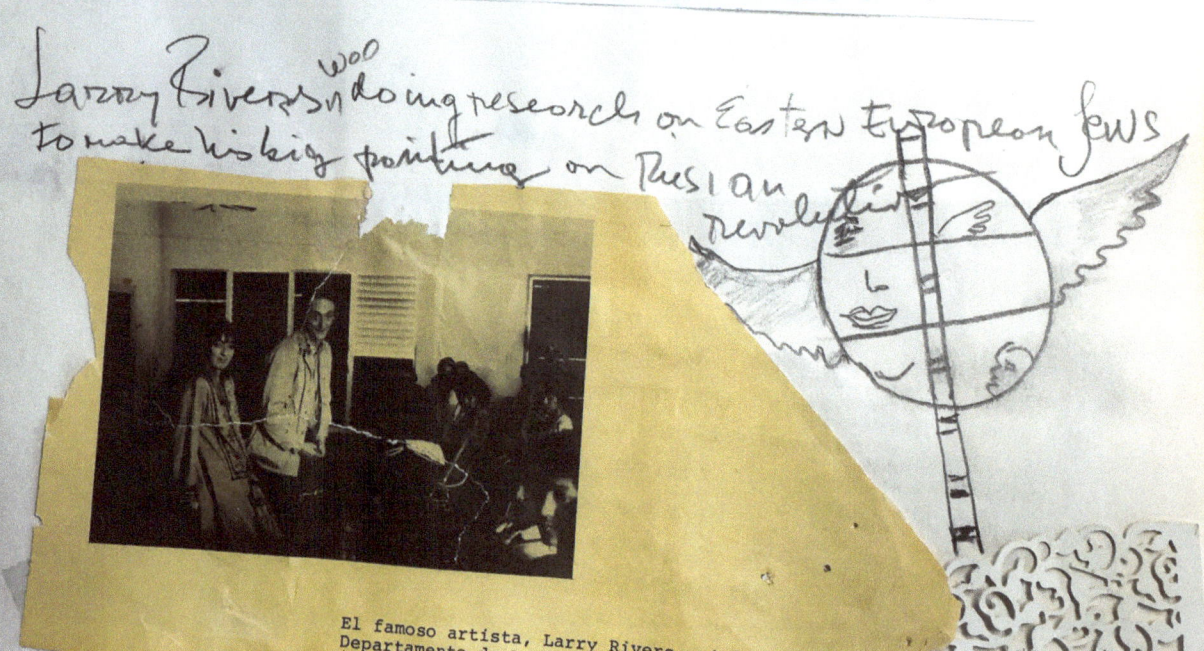

El famoso artista, Larry Rivers, visita nuestro Departamento de Arte. Presenta sus obras y dicta conferencias.

here I am with Larry Rivers at InterAmerican University in P.R. What a wonderful treat!

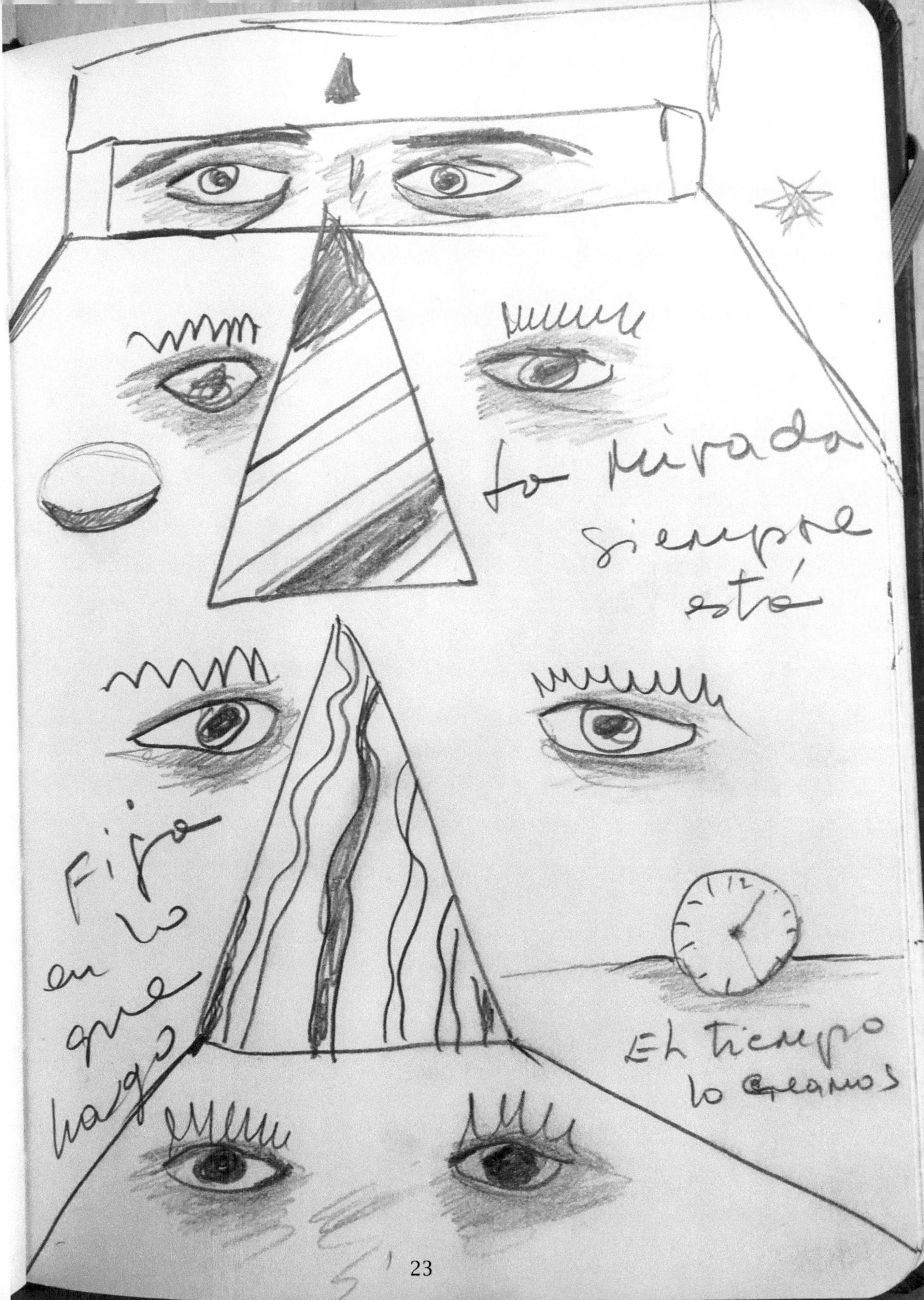

Tu mirada siempre está

Fija en lo que hago

El tiempo lo creamos

Because of all the things you see when your eyes are closed, animals - ecofeminist analysis.
the other side of reality is Myth,

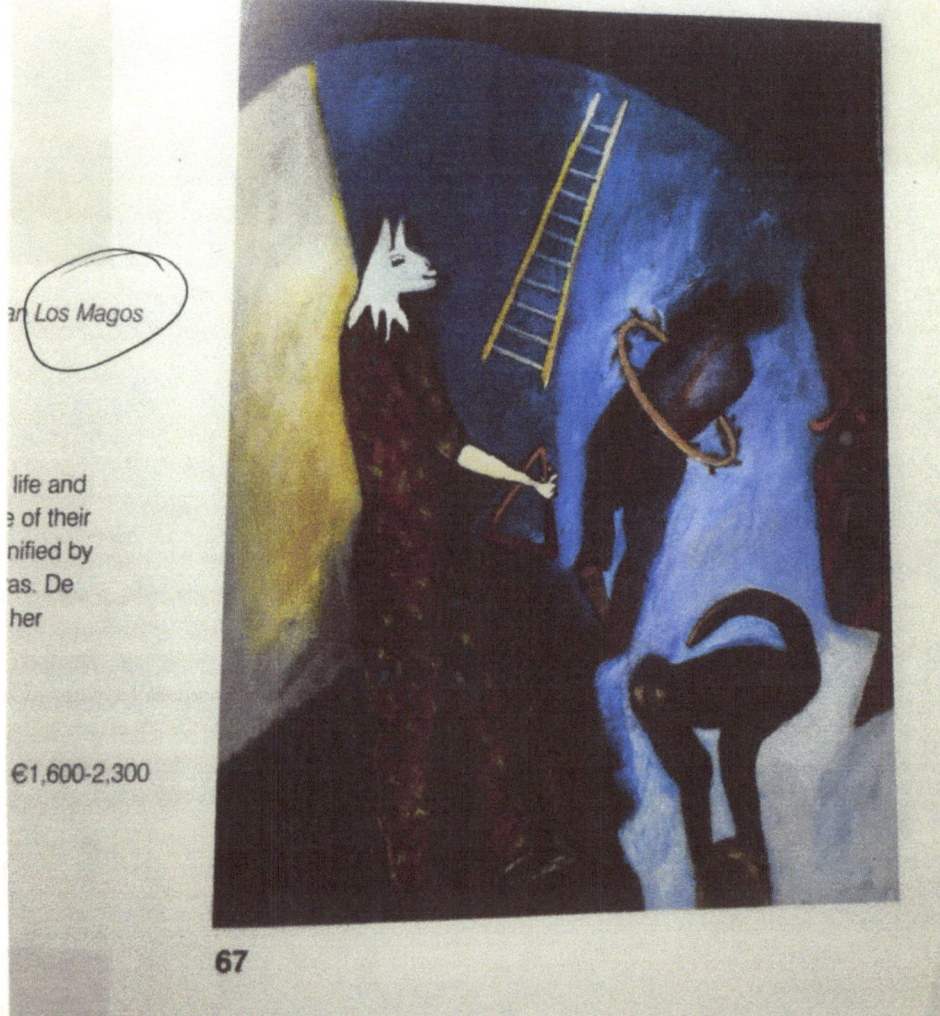

photo from catalogue

My painting at Christie's in London.

to do art you have to be courageous and explore, experiment with ways that are not the expected ones. See things in a different way, stretch the idea and make it your own, add elements from another universe, combine differences and see what happens. Ambiguity is always challenging + interesting. Research, look into things carefully, knowledge is the force of passion in creative work.

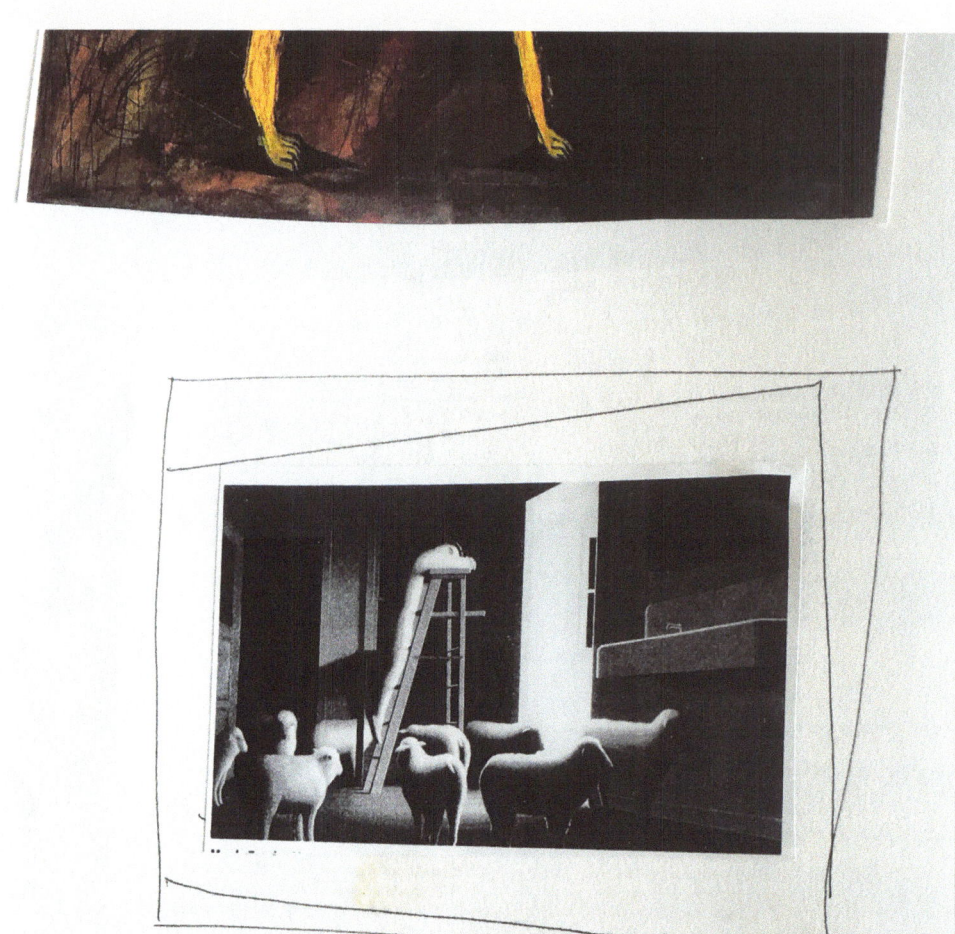

It takes time to perceive, internalize and respond to the aesthetic values in the art of people whose culture differs from ours.

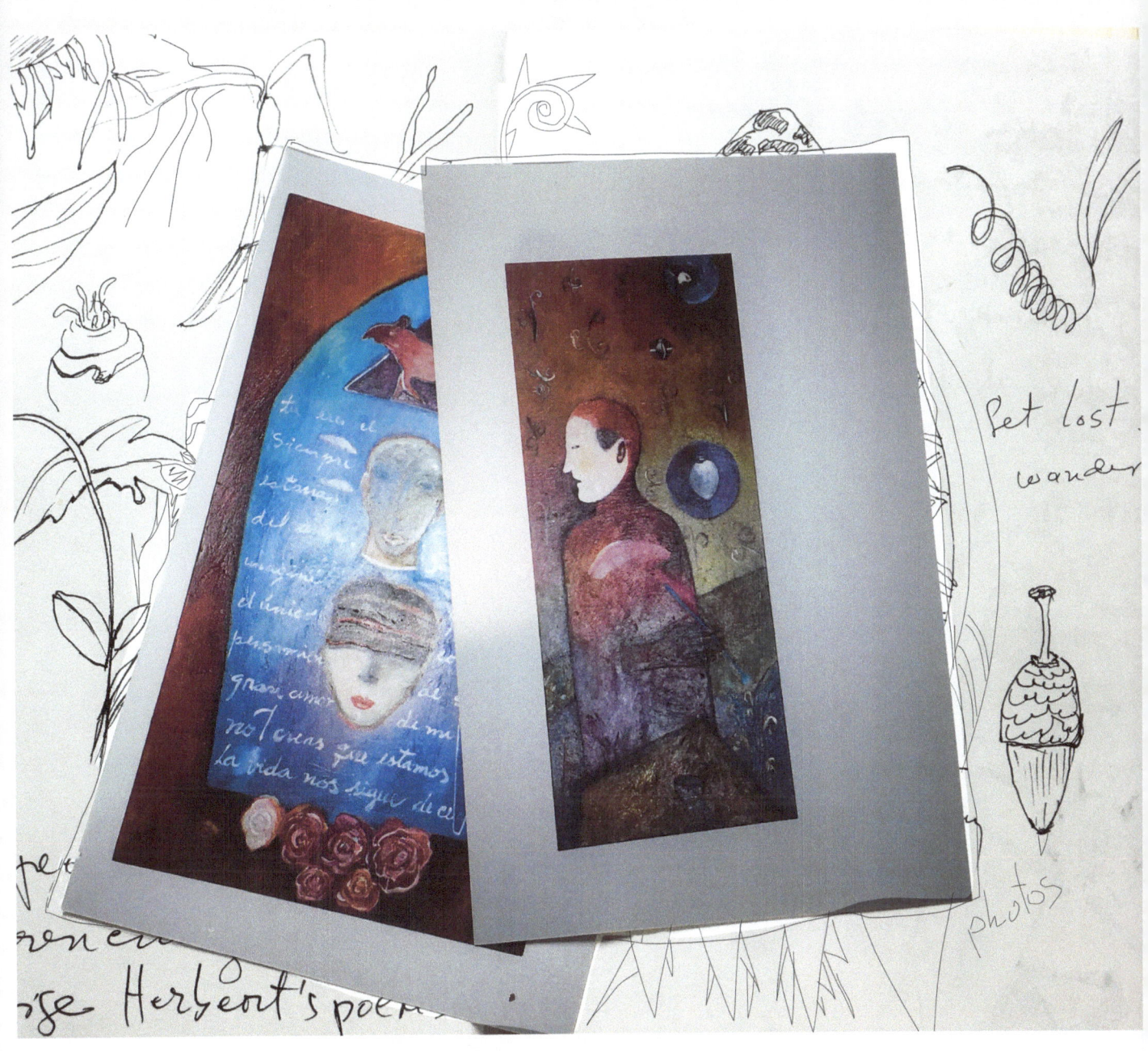

In art familiarity produces appreciation...

> A playwright knows that what is most private in her heart of hearts is also the most astonishing.
>
> —Tina Howe, playwright

Floating angel — symbolizing spiritual dimension in history and people's lives —

the ladder as in Jacob's dream connecting earth + spiritual world —

to reach higher + higher levels of spirituality also stands for the scholarly of sephardi leaders
Isaac Alfassi —
Yehuda Halevi —
Abraham Ibn-Ezra

pomegranate —
rams horn —

wings

photo

MAGEN OVADIA
clle 79 # 9-96
Bogotá —
~~[scribbled out]~~

RUBIES + REBELS. Jewish female
Identity in Contemp. British art
MONICA BOHM-DUCKEN

IMAGE OF GARDEN:
JEWS WERE THE FIRST
people to imagine a
parodise on earth.

Scent, perfume, ideas
all referencing plants
look at George Herbert's
POEMS —

I wonder if the top is based on a plant shape!

> After leaving school students often don't work because there's no reason to work. Nobody pays attention any more: so there seems no reason to press on.
> —Bruce Boice, painter

BEESWAX — embeded c cosas - fotos? embedding notemas/
originals.

☐ — color suave debajo.

silent garden — intimate archaeological sits - alambre

the extinction piece - historia or photos
press seeds on paper - flores

GASA

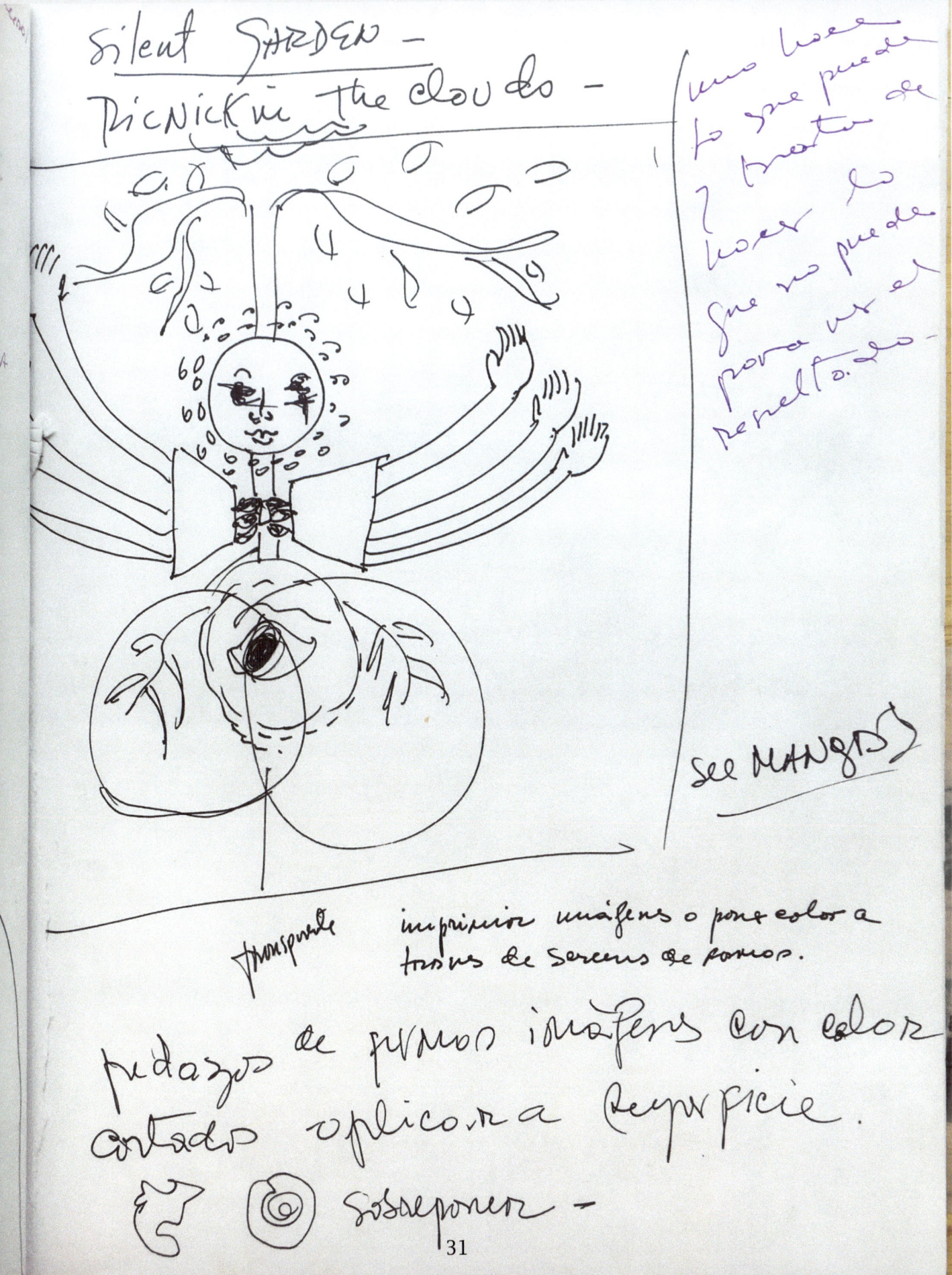

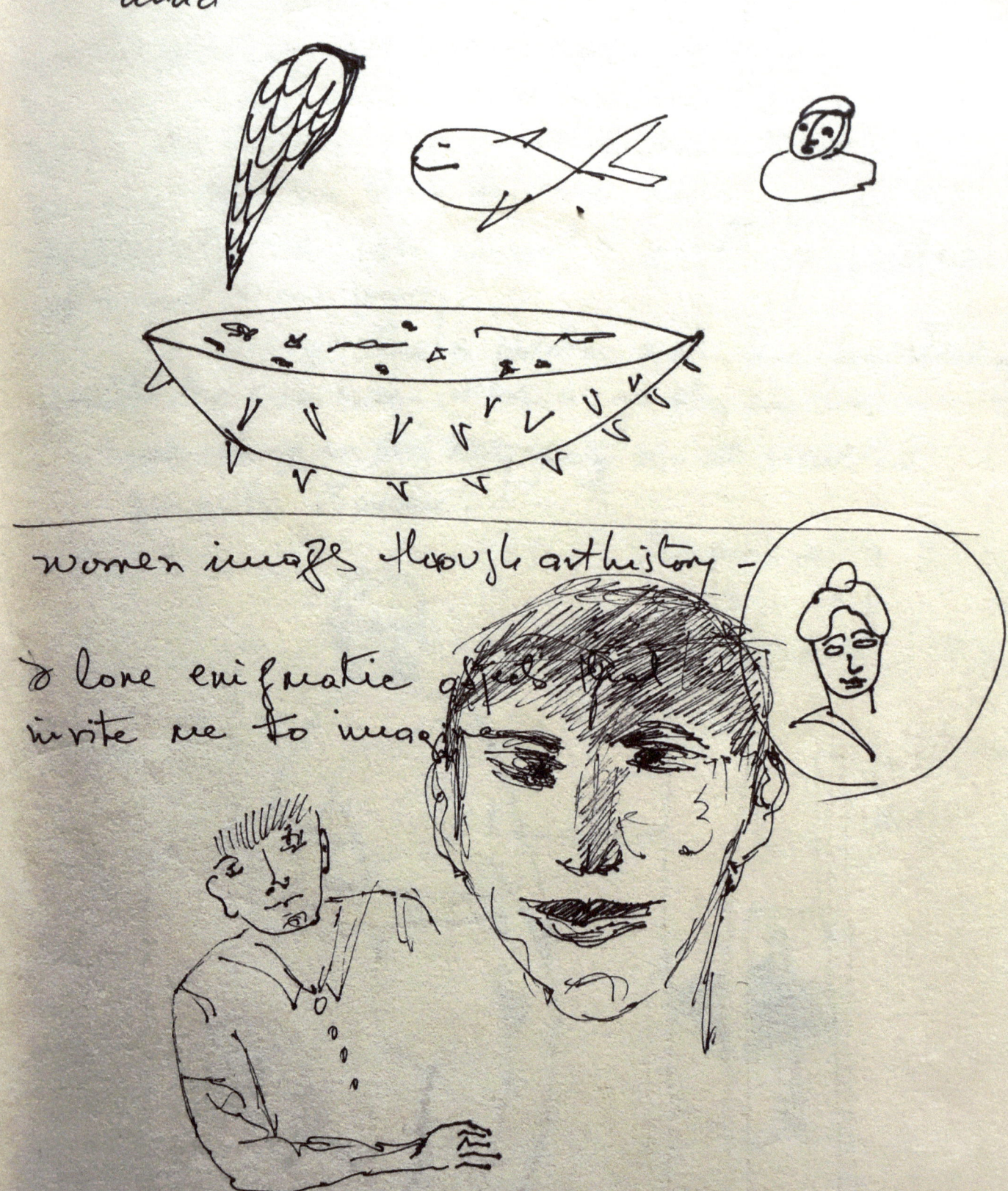

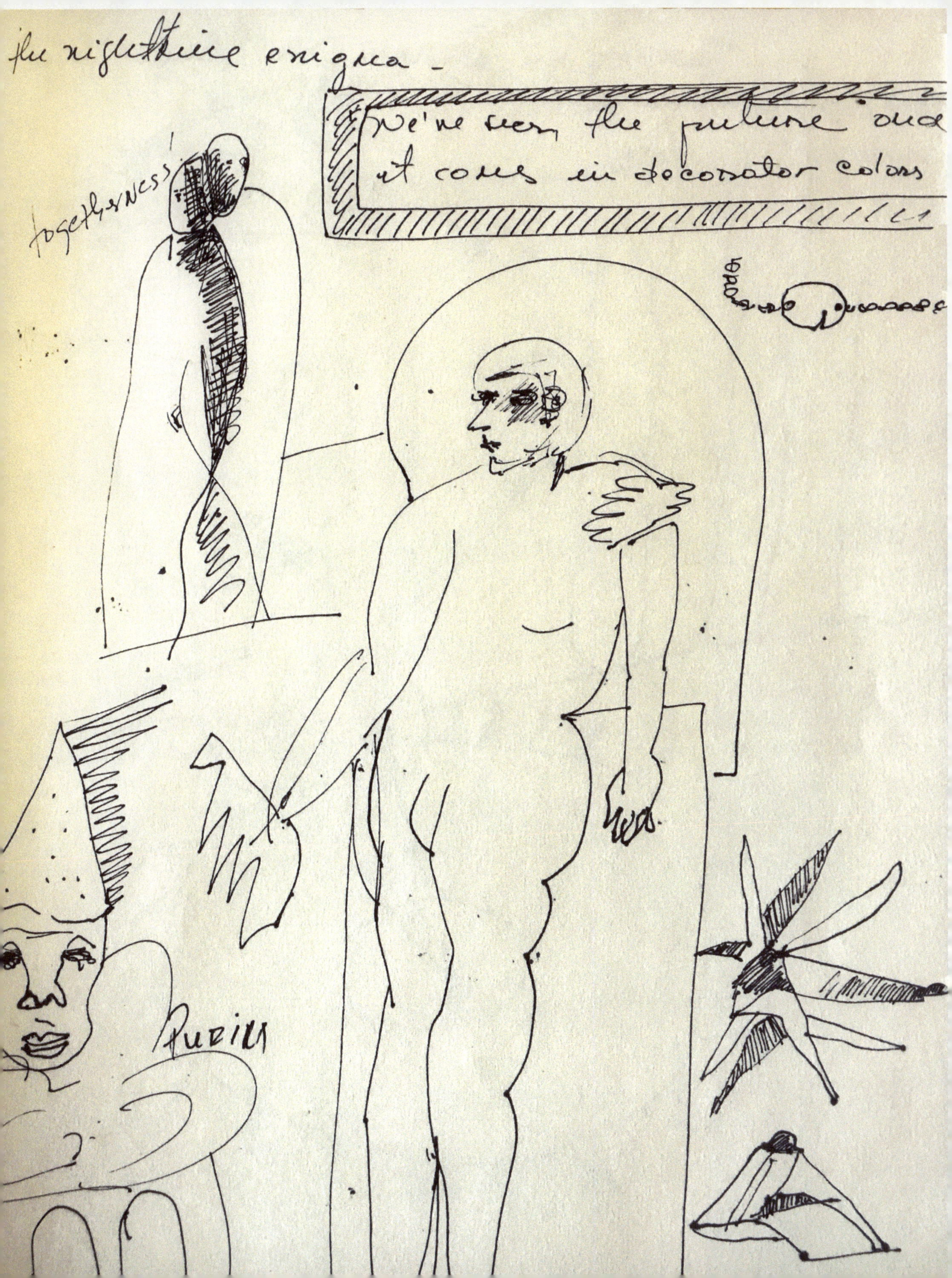

the nighttime enigma –

togetherness!

we've seen the future and
it comes in decorator colors

We feel paralized sometimes.... the best way to loosen up is to just scratch the paper with lines which develop in thoughts that become images. these images bring to mind other visions and concepts to tickle the imagination and continue the process.

Acrylic, graphlite + coffee on folded paper.

Charcoal on paper - primero pintar de gesso con graphlite luego charcoal -

Fragments make life

Foots and other icons

La noche del tapir -

Kiddush

I never force
devout sentiment
and never
compose hymns or
prayers except
when I am
involuntarily
overwhelmed by it,
so it is usually
a real, genuine
devoutness.
—Franz Schubert,
composer

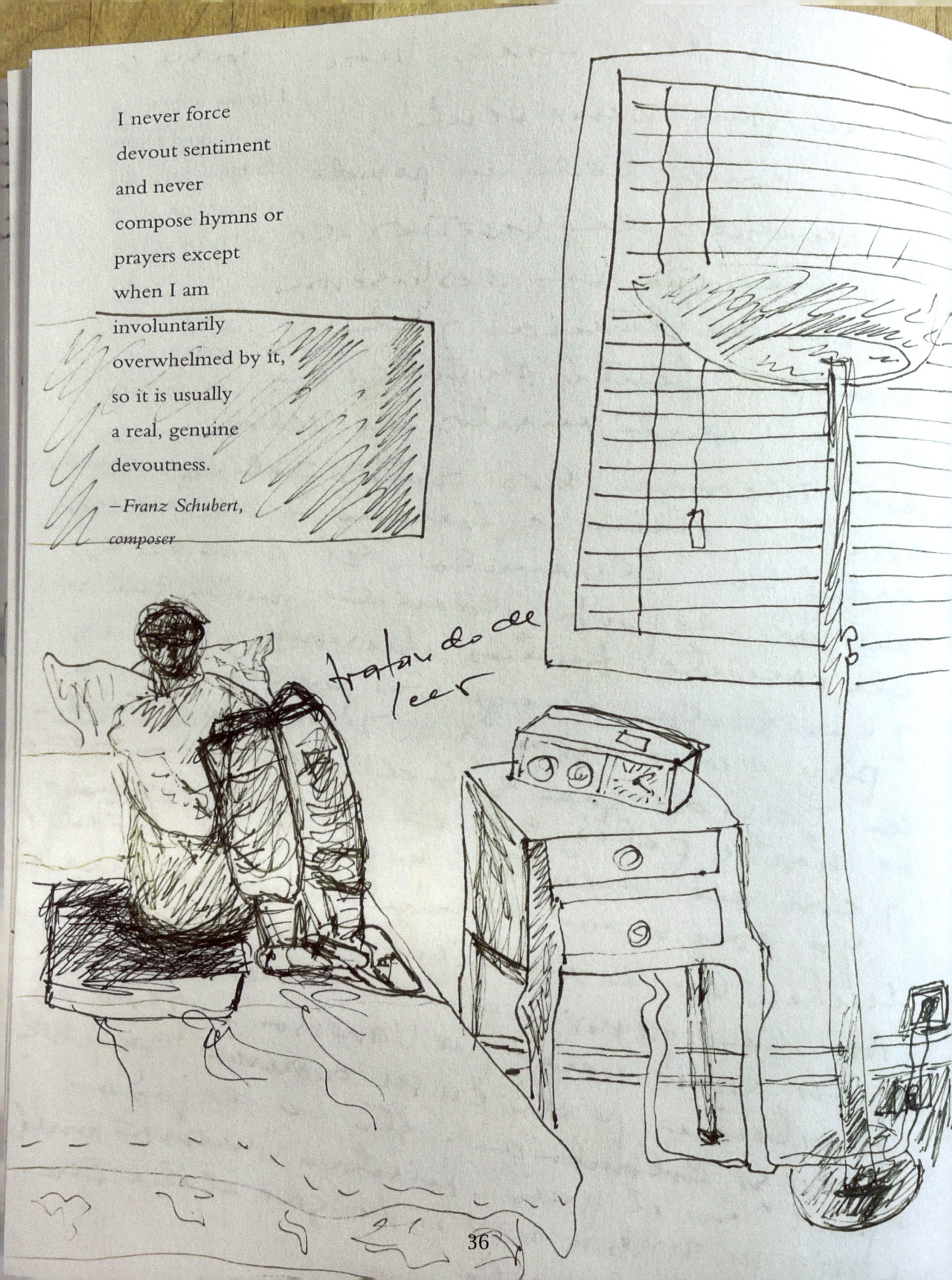

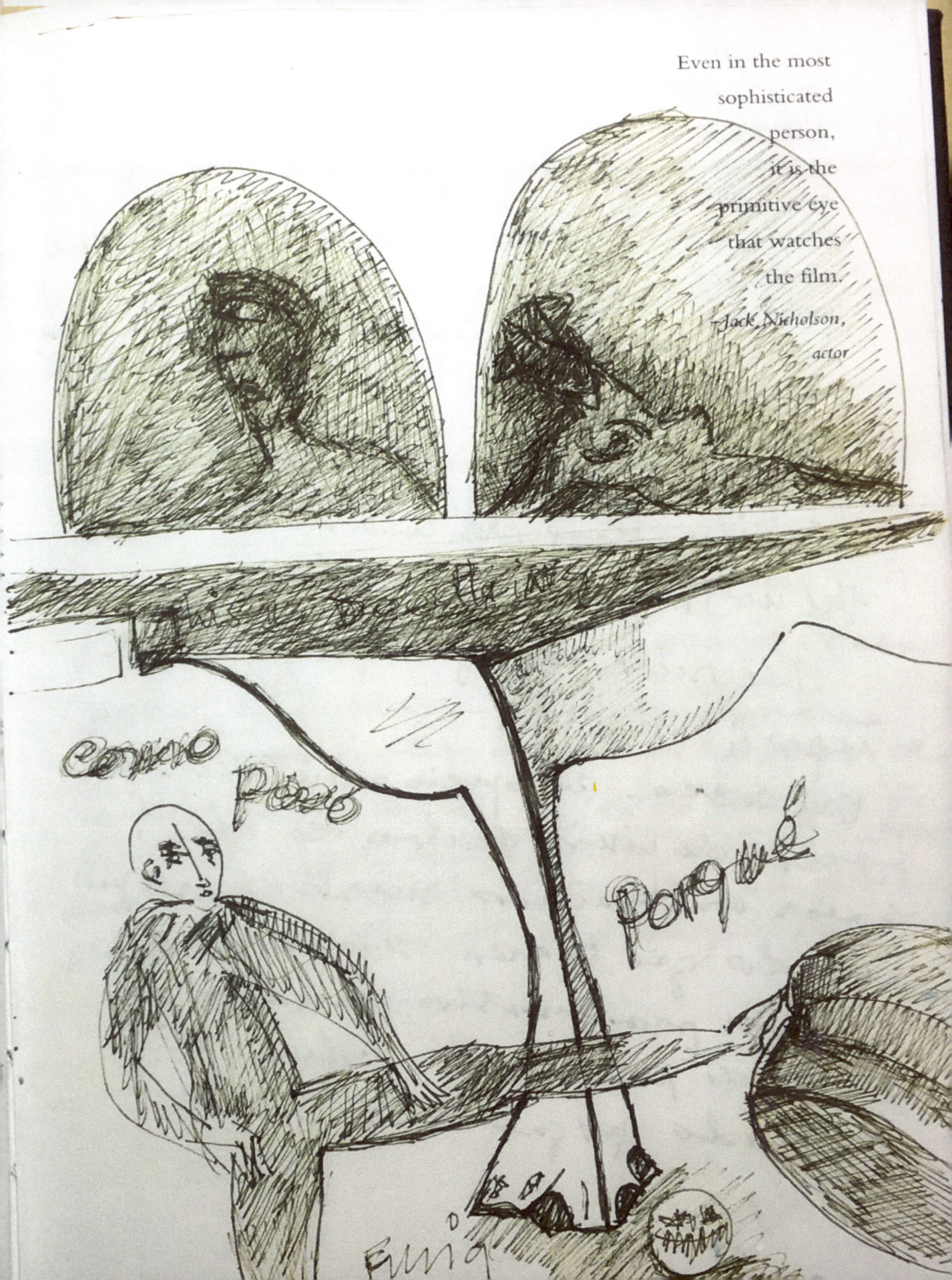

Even in the most sophisticated person, it is the primitive eye that watches the film.
Jack Nicholson, actor

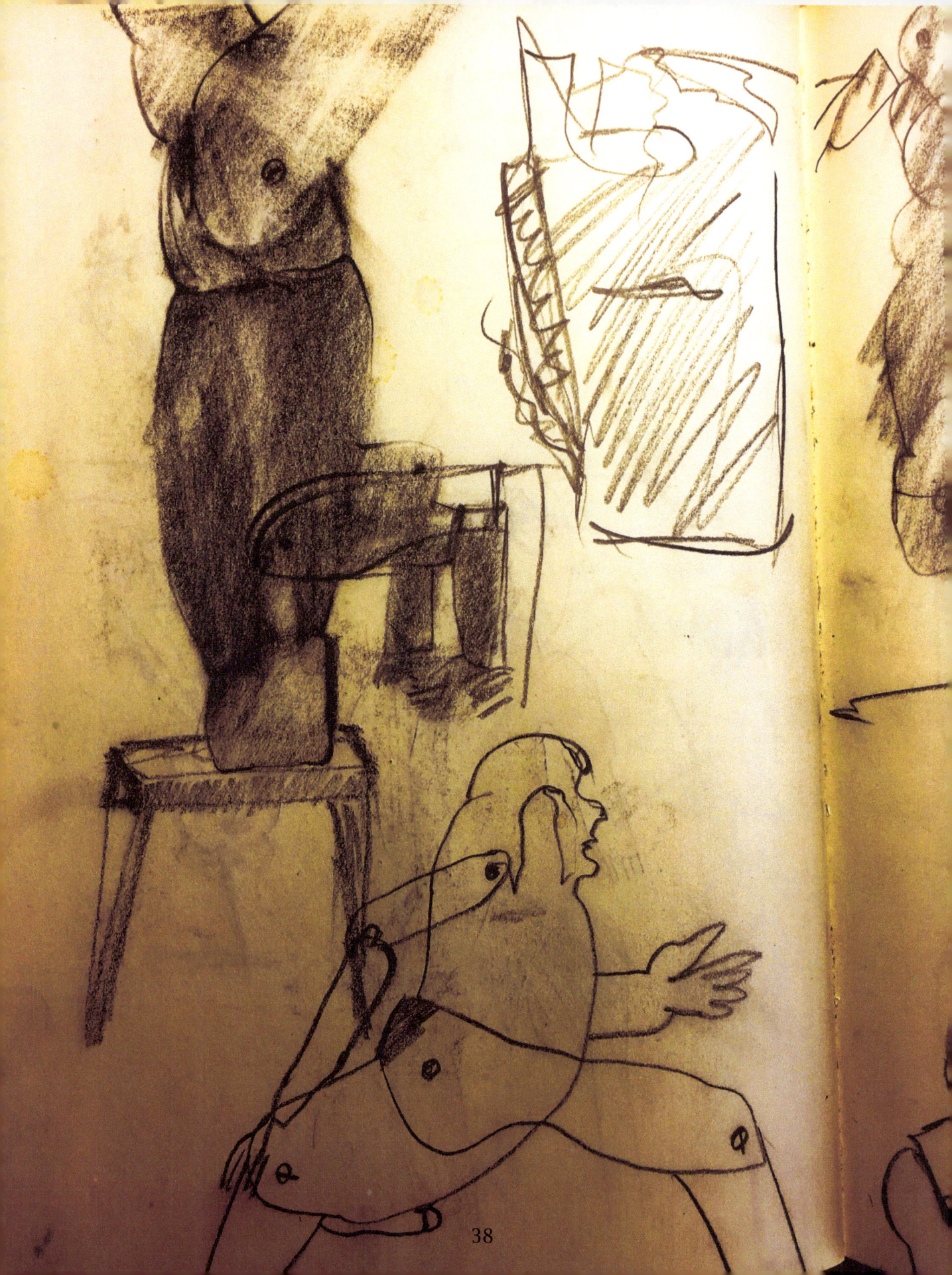

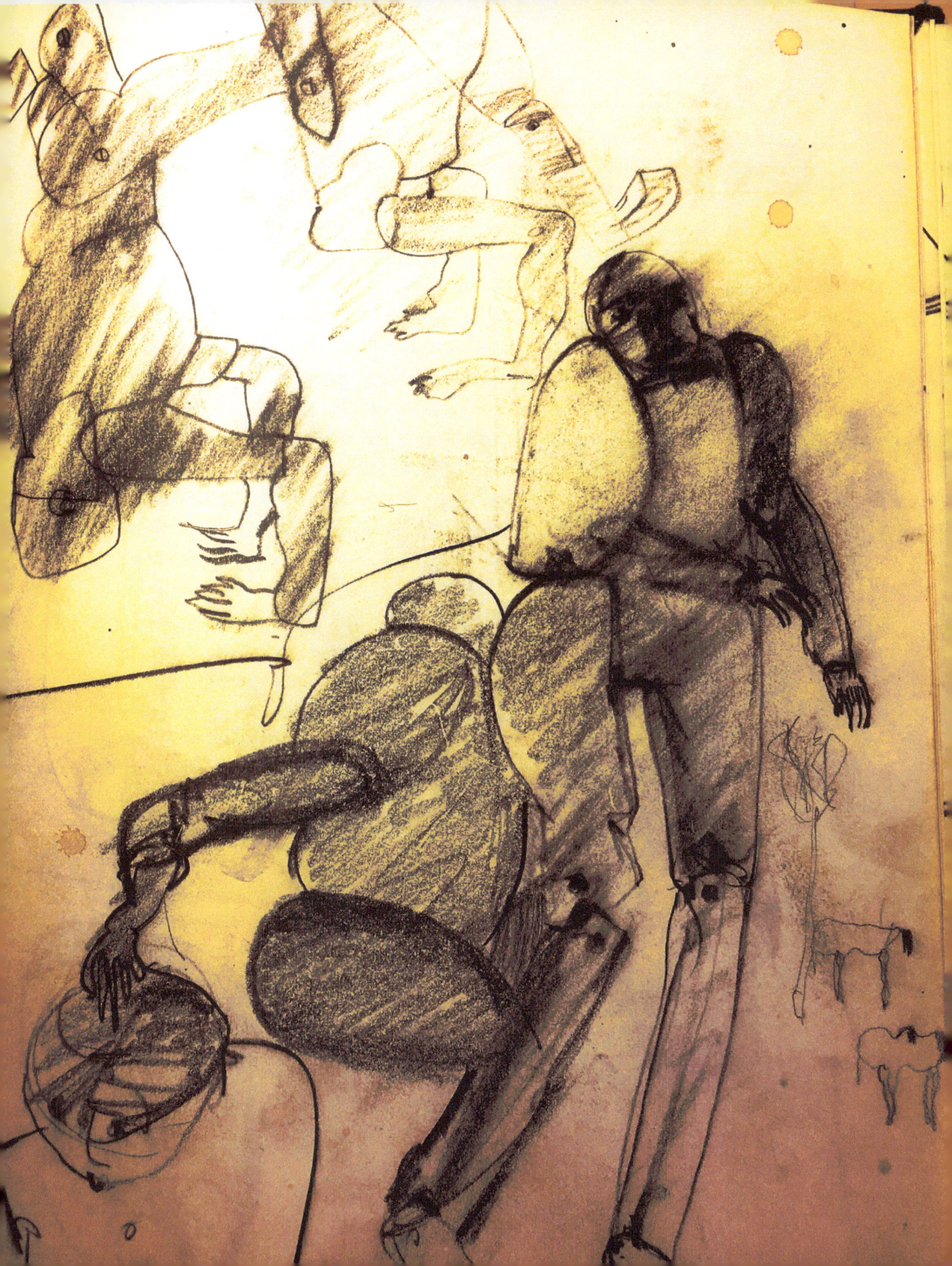

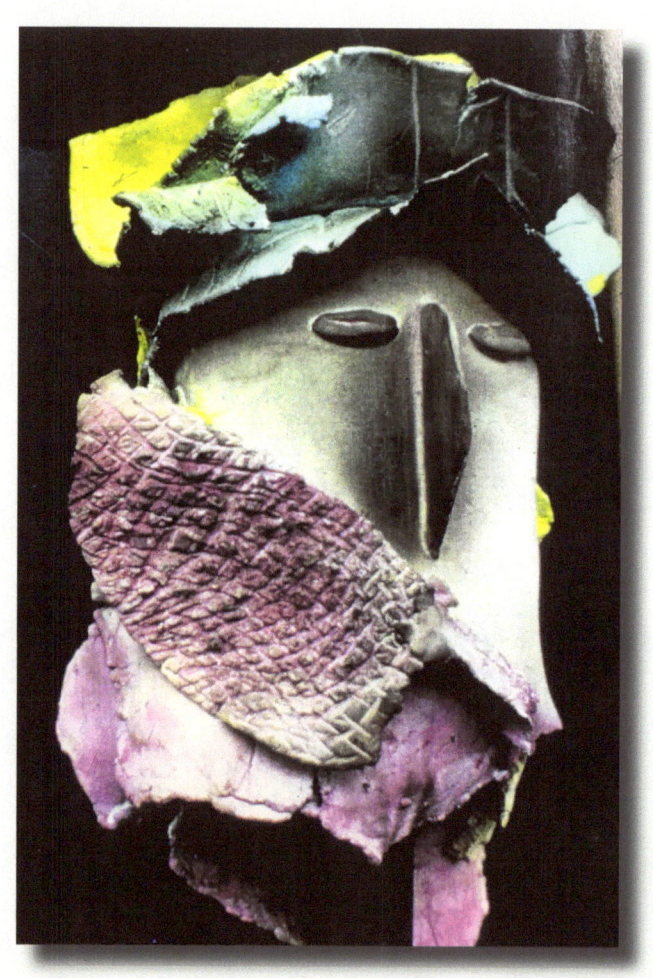

*Doing art is an exaltation of the senses.
How does that process emerge?
Dreams, images, fantasies, observation, words.*

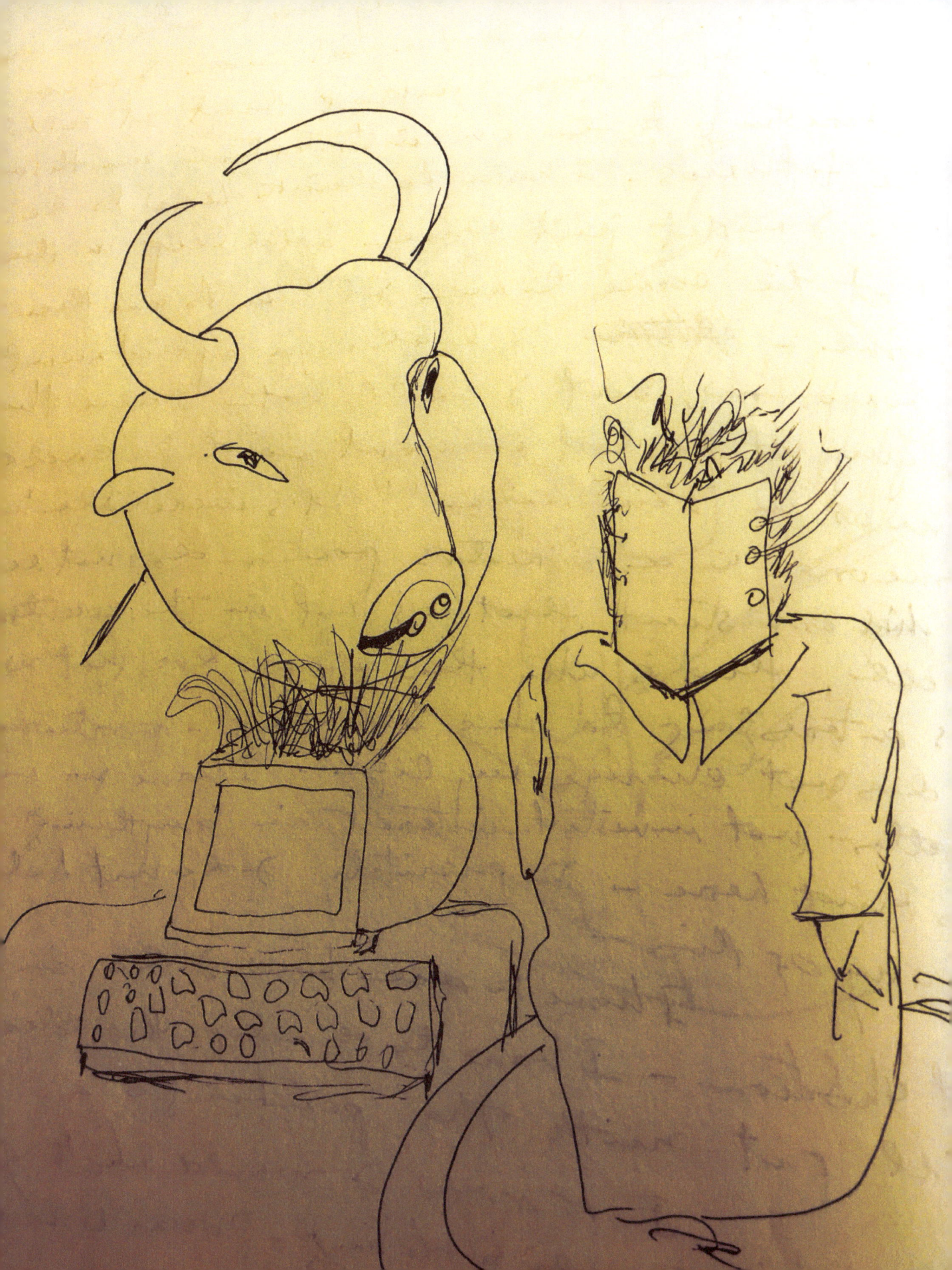

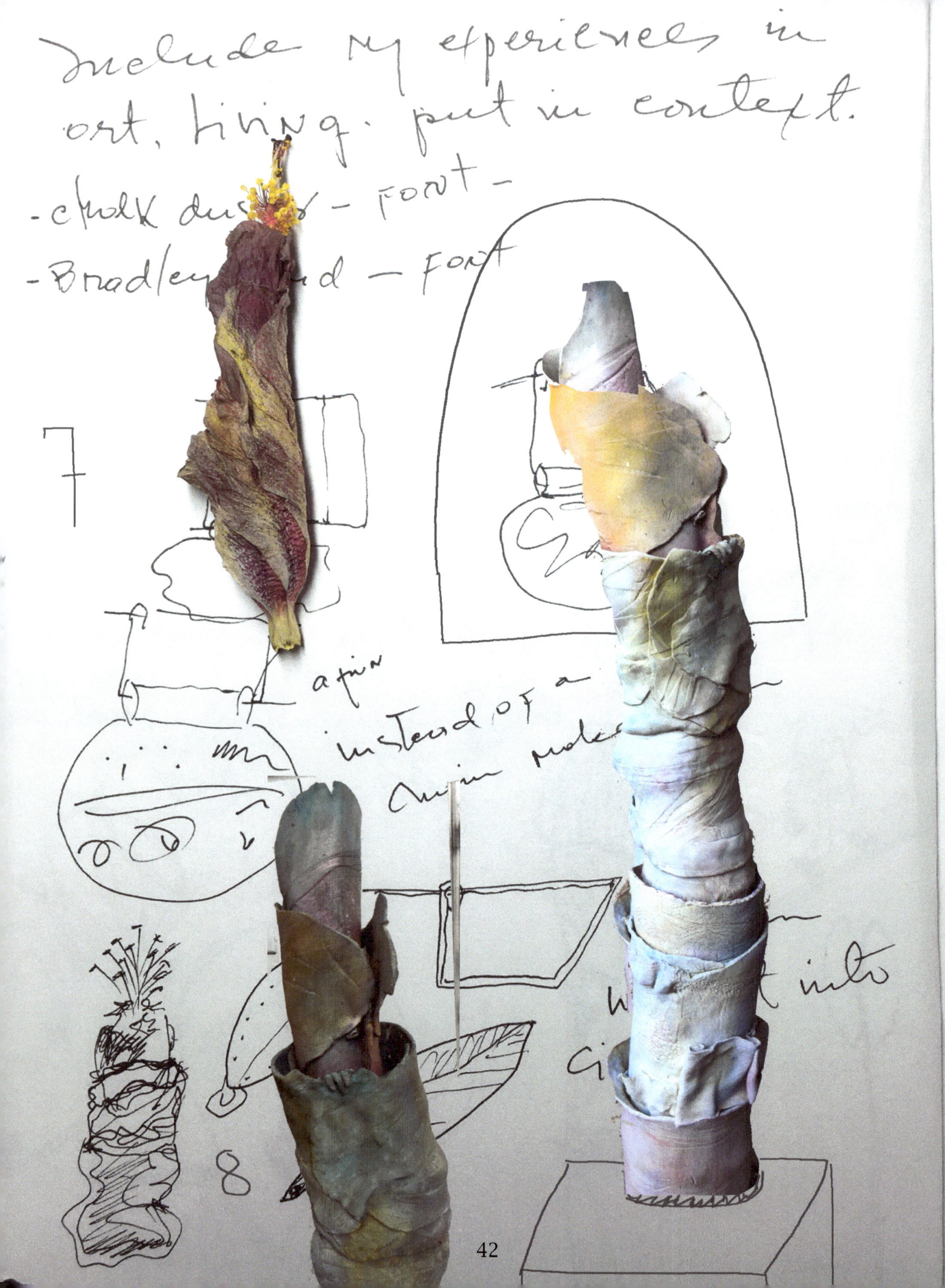

Include my experiences in
art, living. put in context.
- chalk dust — font —
- Bradley ____ — font

a pin
instead of a
___ ____

8

42

Color associations are culturally important and historically tell us about people's views. In the 19th c. Green was associated with poison and bad luck because it was made with arsenic! but associations keep changing. Green is now associated with ecology and nature preservation.

Green is good! Green is calming...

By doing ceramics I understood the chemical complexity of color and how it was affected by heat. Raw Siena that I used in acrylic paintings, when doing ceramics I realized it was a combination of Red Iron oxide, caolin and feldspar. What a wonderful magical thing it was the result!

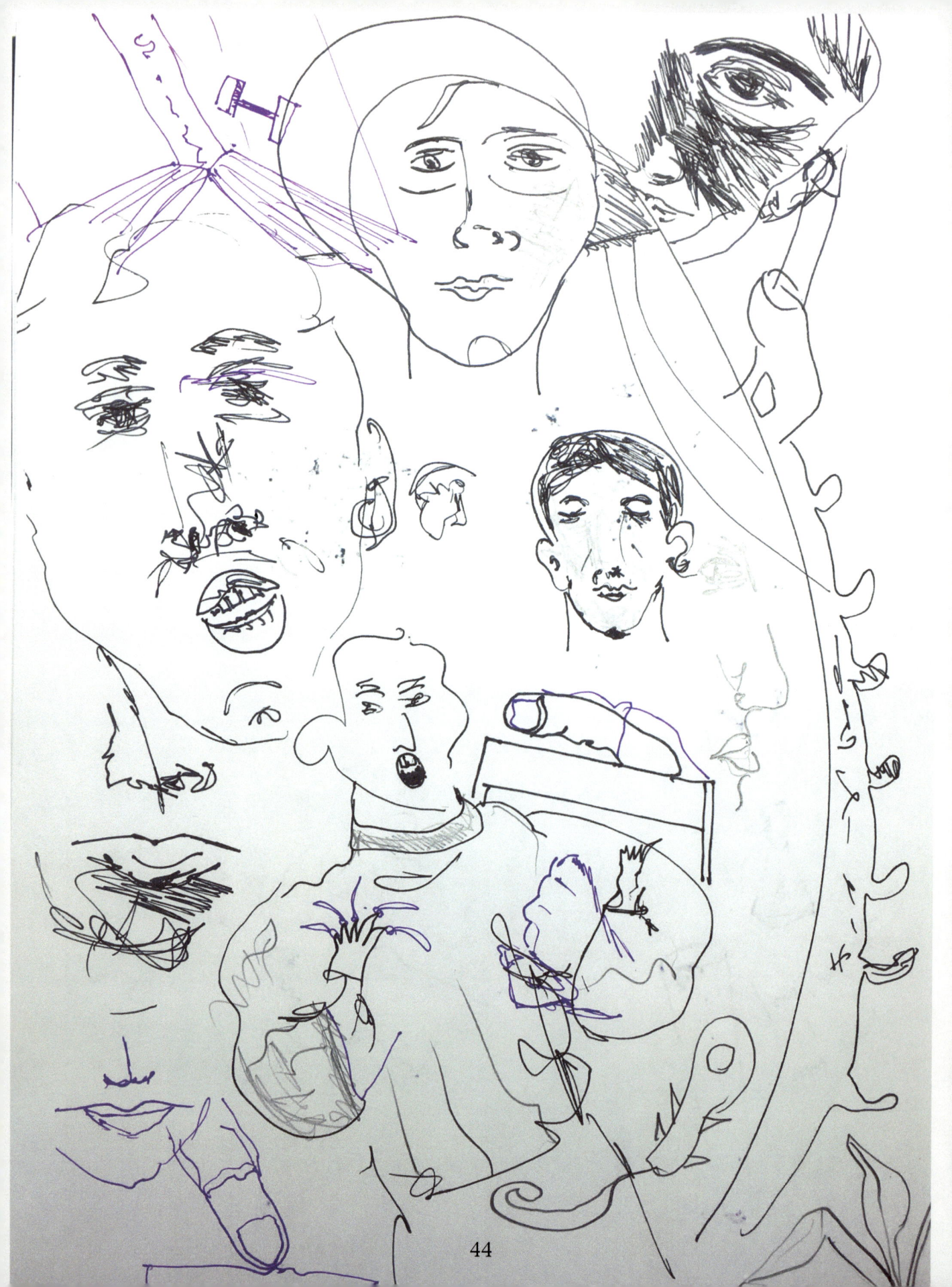

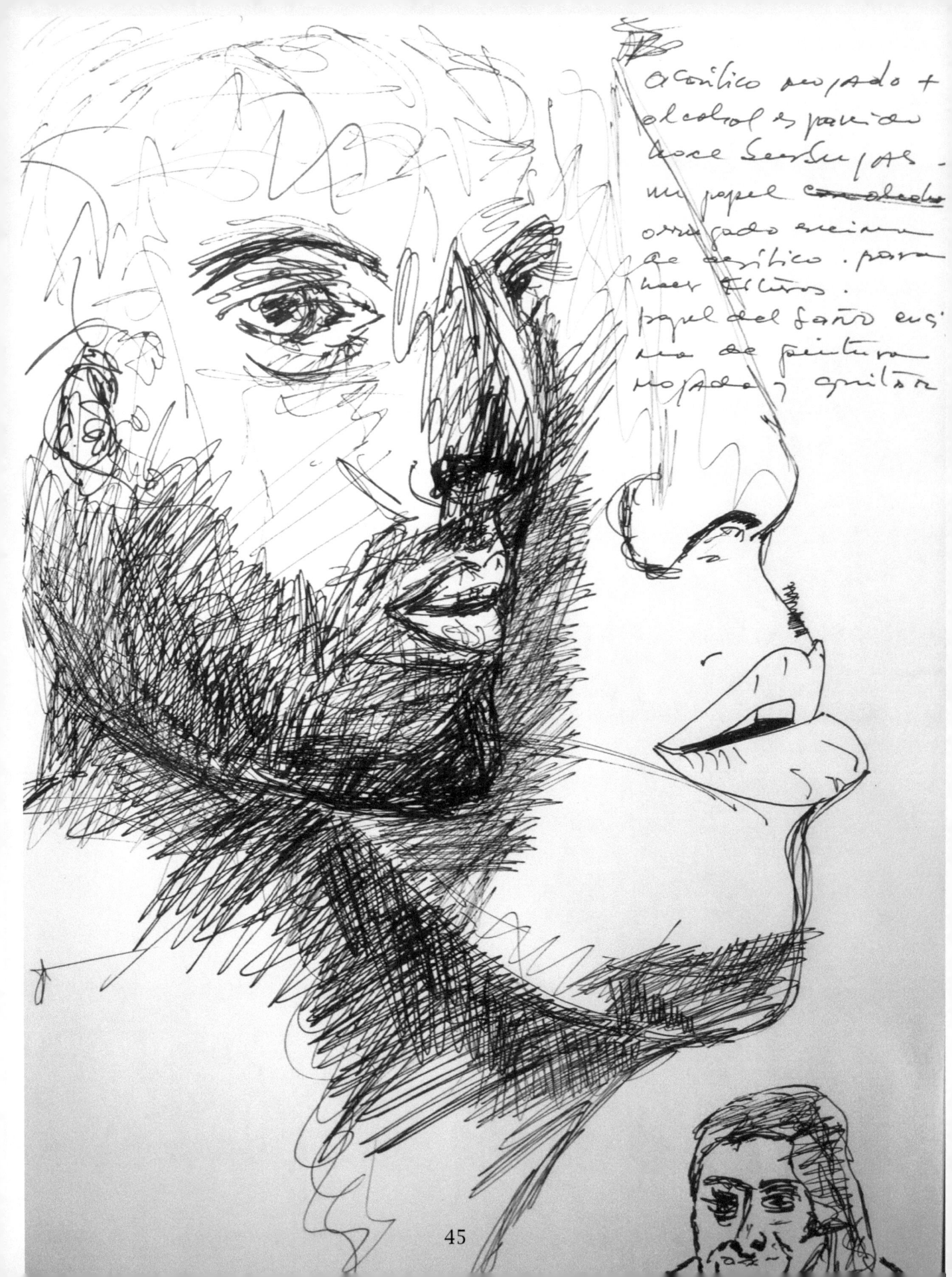

doodling with art history...

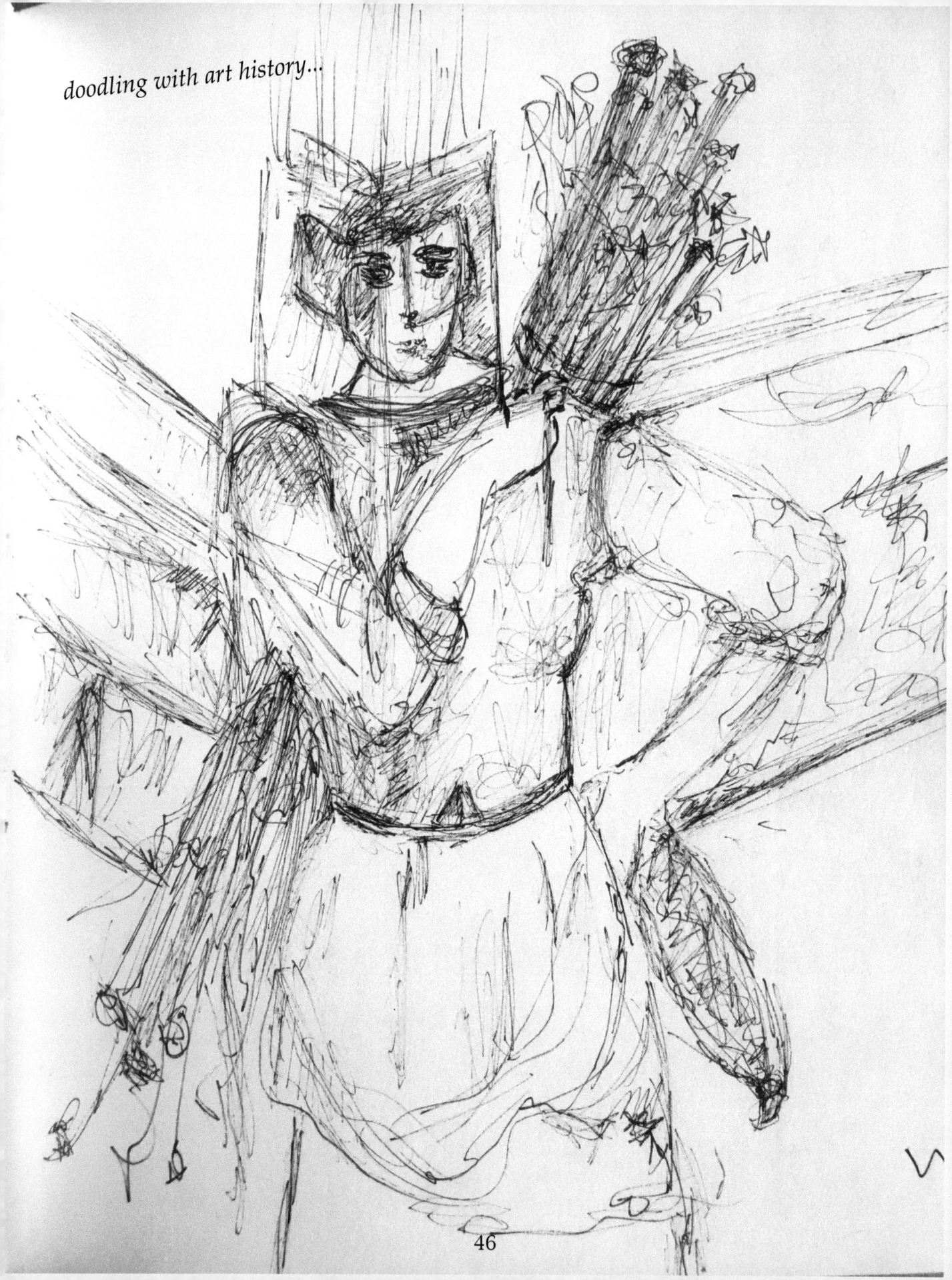

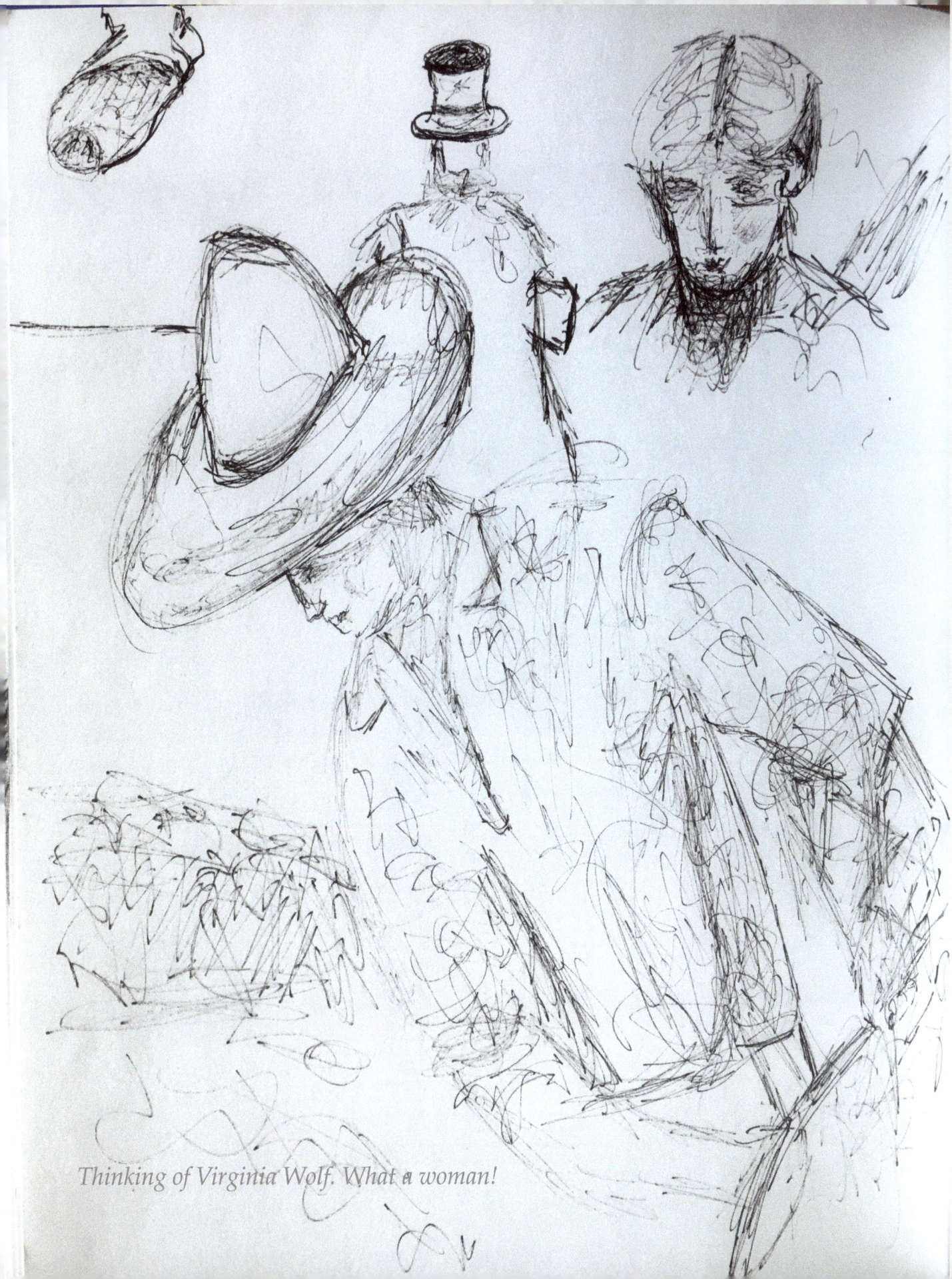
Thinking of Virginia Wolf. What a woman!

Borges y la metáfora

Ocaso — vejez
Flores — Mujer
Estrellas — Ver —
Río — tiempo.

"Elegía del Recuerdo Imposible"

¿Qué es el tiempo?

Te amaré eternamente y aún más!

La vida nos sigue de cerca!

Memory is made of images —

a metaphore suggest images —

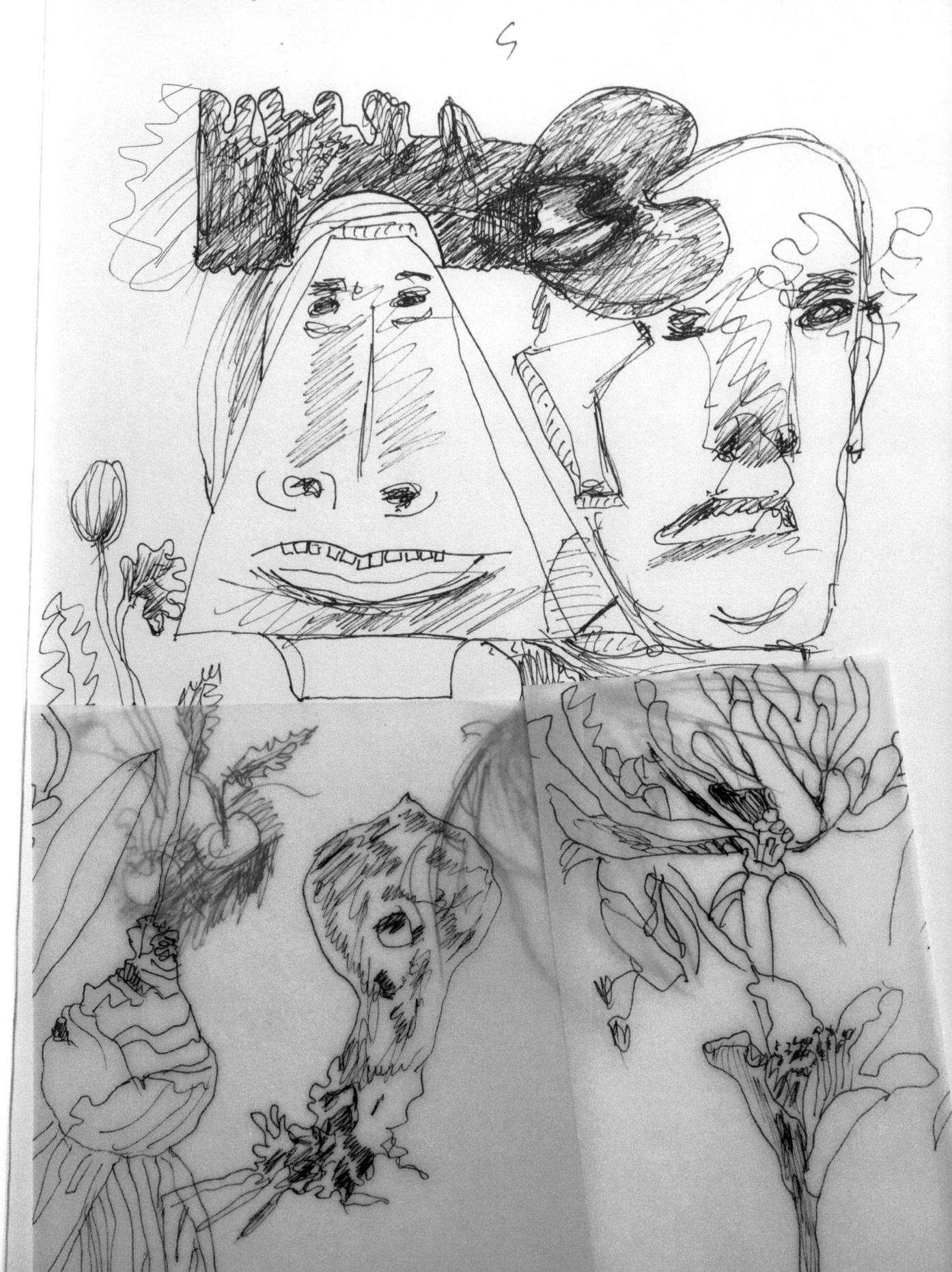

Los fuerzos de mona lisa
Estan en todos partes como
será que hemos estado influenciados
por tantos años tal be imagenes hacer algo mejor
es casi imposible rector es las cosa

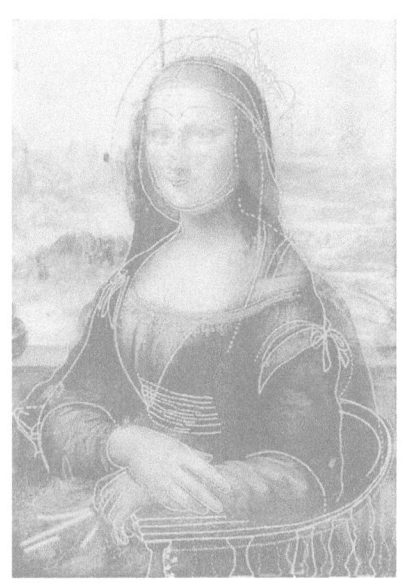

The strength of the Mona Lisa's image is always present in Western iconography. It has made its appearance even in popular music as in Cole Porter's "You're the Top" where he equates the smile with fabulous things as Camembert cheese...

We have been so influenced by centuries of images that to do something new is almost impossible.
To remember is the thing...

—Lance Morrow, *writer*

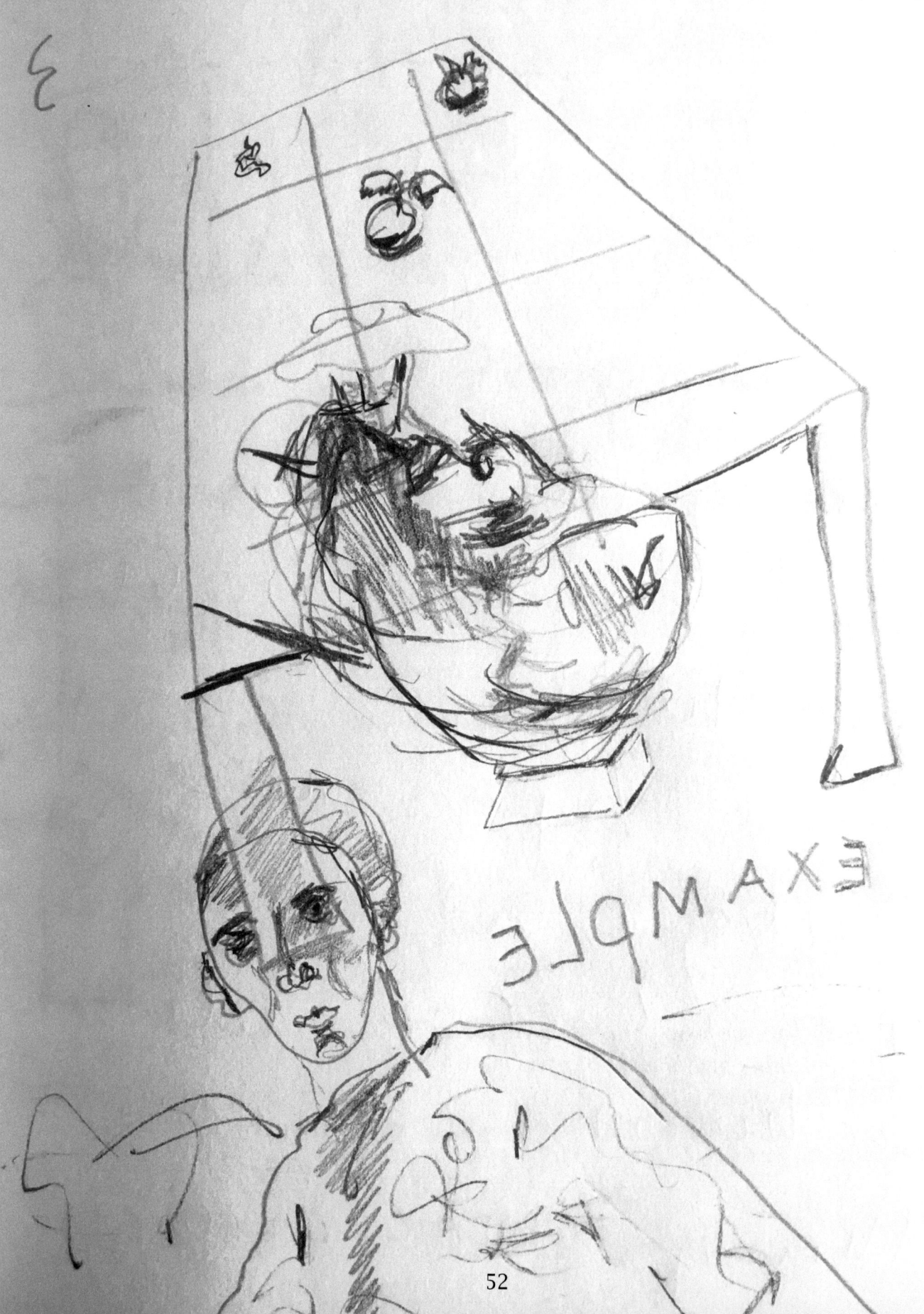

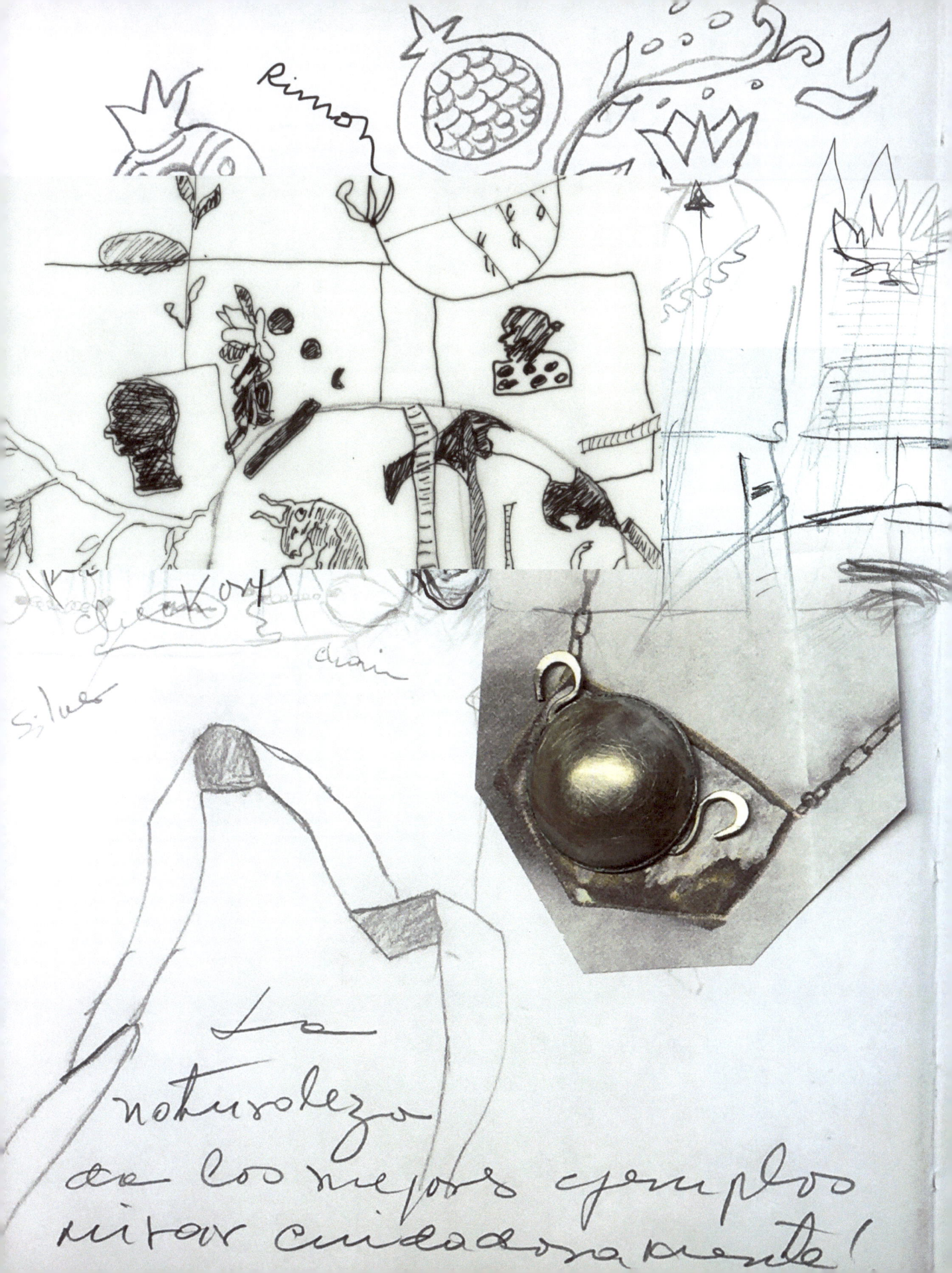

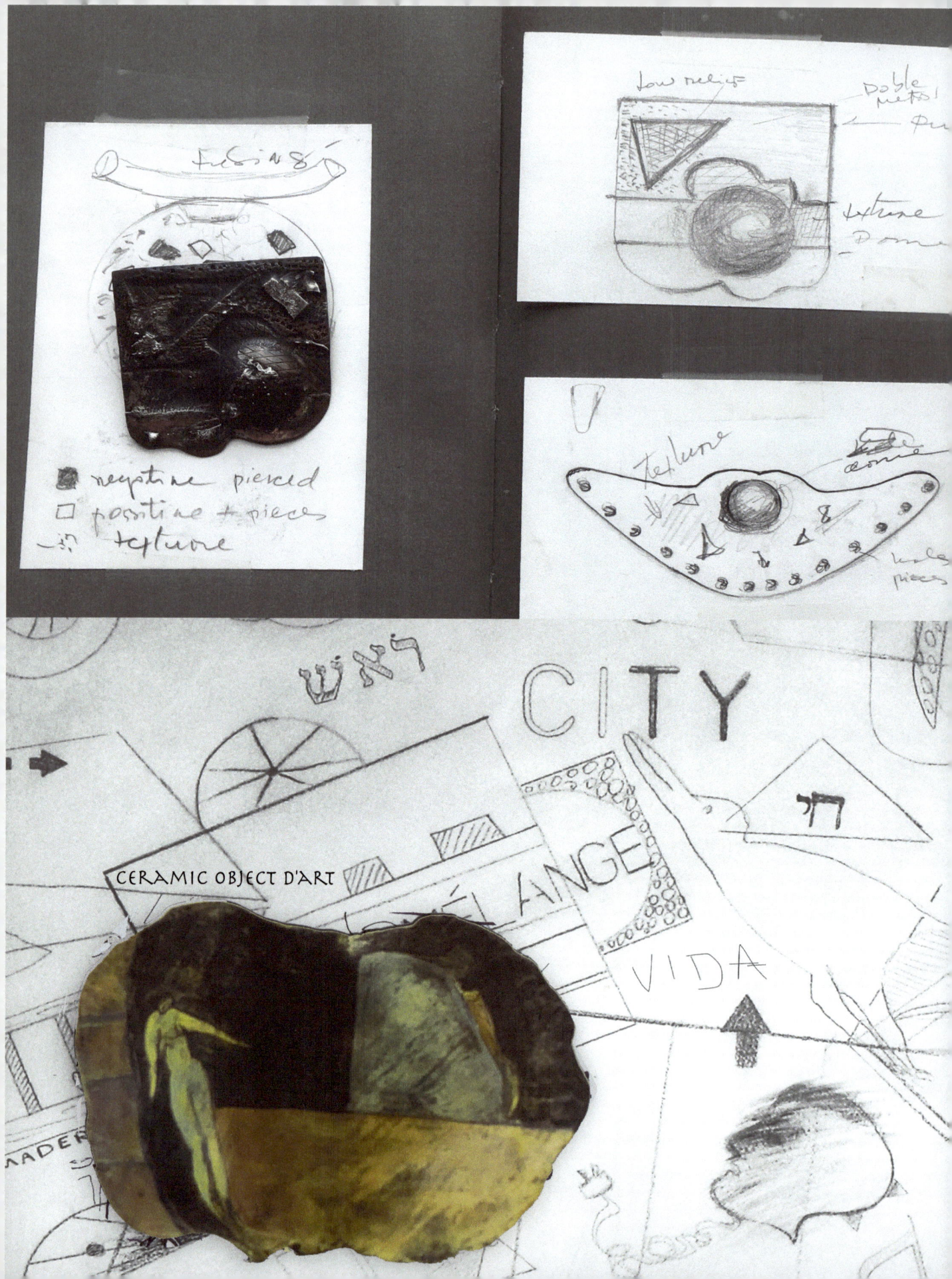

CERAMIC OBJECT D'ART

aute
medio doblado
con pespuntes a ela

I always see the poetic potential of objects.
To deconstruct them or what they signify and make something else that might or might not relate to them.

What is poetry if not the essence of feeling?
There's poetry in looking when you catch the essence of that which you are looking...
a sunset or the Alba.

rabbi -
Juda alHarizi - 1165 Toledo 12
traveled to Jerusalem 1216

thinking about creativity. Let your mind be free travel through time if you look at what is close to your space... examine it in detail

18 12

the creative hand that protects controls babars and directs. que haria sin poder utilizar la manos the hand does what my mind holds. If I could only reproduce my mind in drawing

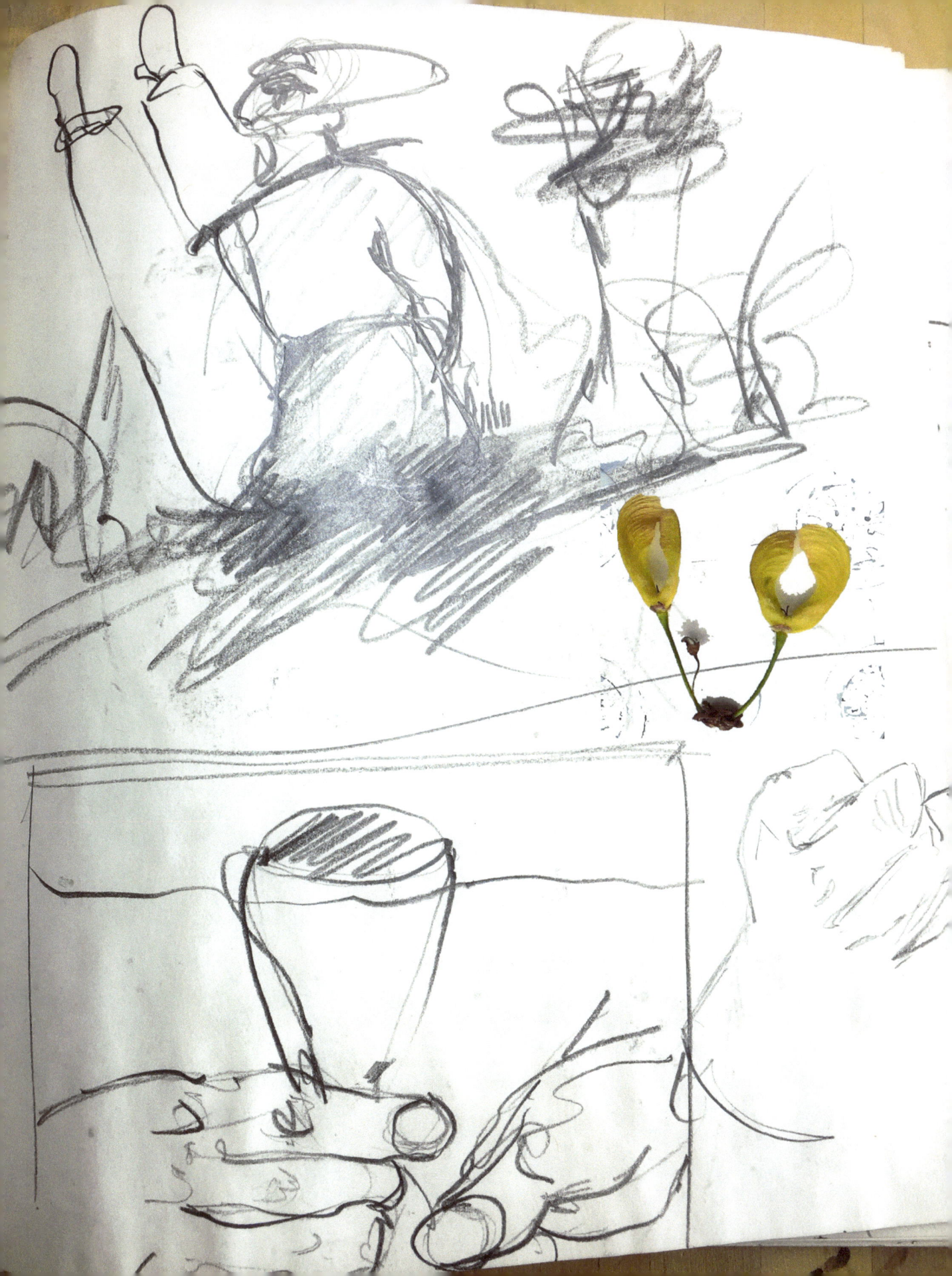

IBN Gabirol - was alone with his soul - his interior was producing poetry - "yo te voy a buscar en el alba" - IBN Gabirol -

IBN Gabirol - writes his poems in both Hebrew + Arabic - simultaneously -

MATUZ Beatruz - el bordado -
_____

Bilingüe - Arabe
                 Hebreo
poema   Prose - Hebreo -

la amada - El Divan -

La teología del deseo —
Ibn Gabirol —
El manantial de la vida,
La fluidez en la creación
Philon — 1º filósofo judío
neoplatónico.

MAHZOR OF WORMS — bird heads —
lack of characteristic beak — nose too,

Bible of ALBA — RABBI MOSES ARRAGEL
513 folios 334 miniatures — commentary
~~Christian artists~~ rabbinic writings on
TARGUMIM, MIDRASHIM + TALMUD but

Also from later who like the Zohar
Rabbi Kloss gave detail instruction to
artists on the illustrations. furnishing them with
special jewish interpret. of biblical scenes. Cain
kills ABEL by biting his neck like a snake like described
in the ZOHAR. Nestri jewish manuscript in
1430 in MAQUEDA — ~~both in toledo~~
rashi nicoli' inspired illuminators
in the great library of the
LIRIA PALACE seat of grand Duke of
Alba and Berwick.

the oldest known liturgical text is a
Spanish MAHZOR - in Hebrew script published
in Portugal around 1485 which include
ritual instruction

the oldest known document is a
treatise on the art of illumination
from 1262. written in Portuguese with
Hebrew characters "O livro de como se
fazem as cores". the instructions
contain in the text use for the illumination
of the Bible manuscript in Coreña
Golicia in 1476

carpet page of
Kennicott Bible
Biblia de la Coruna

other older texts —

A Spanish prayer B/C from 15th century
with portuguese instructions at Bodleian

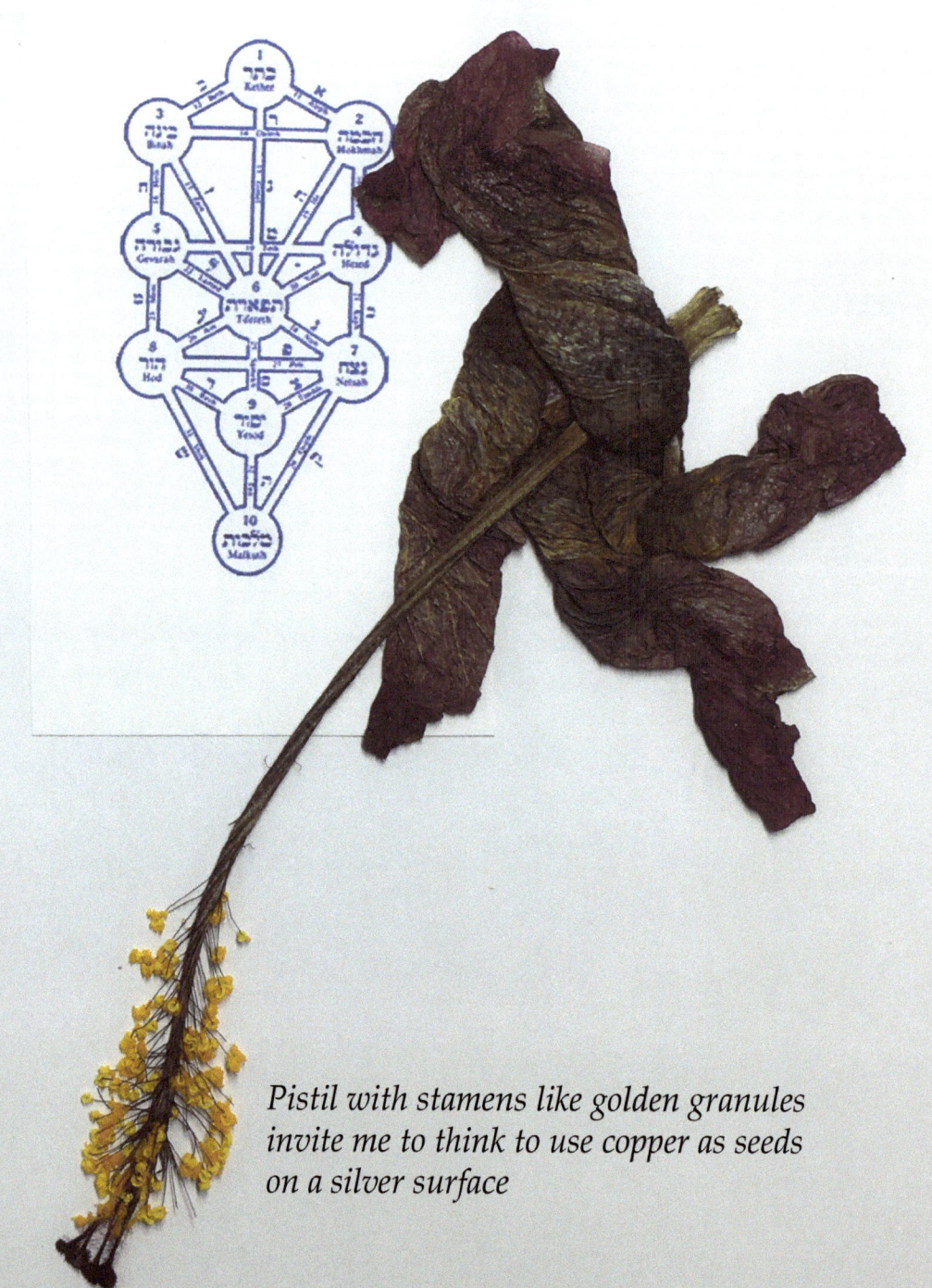

Pistil with stamens like golden granules invite me to think to use copper as seeds on a silver surface

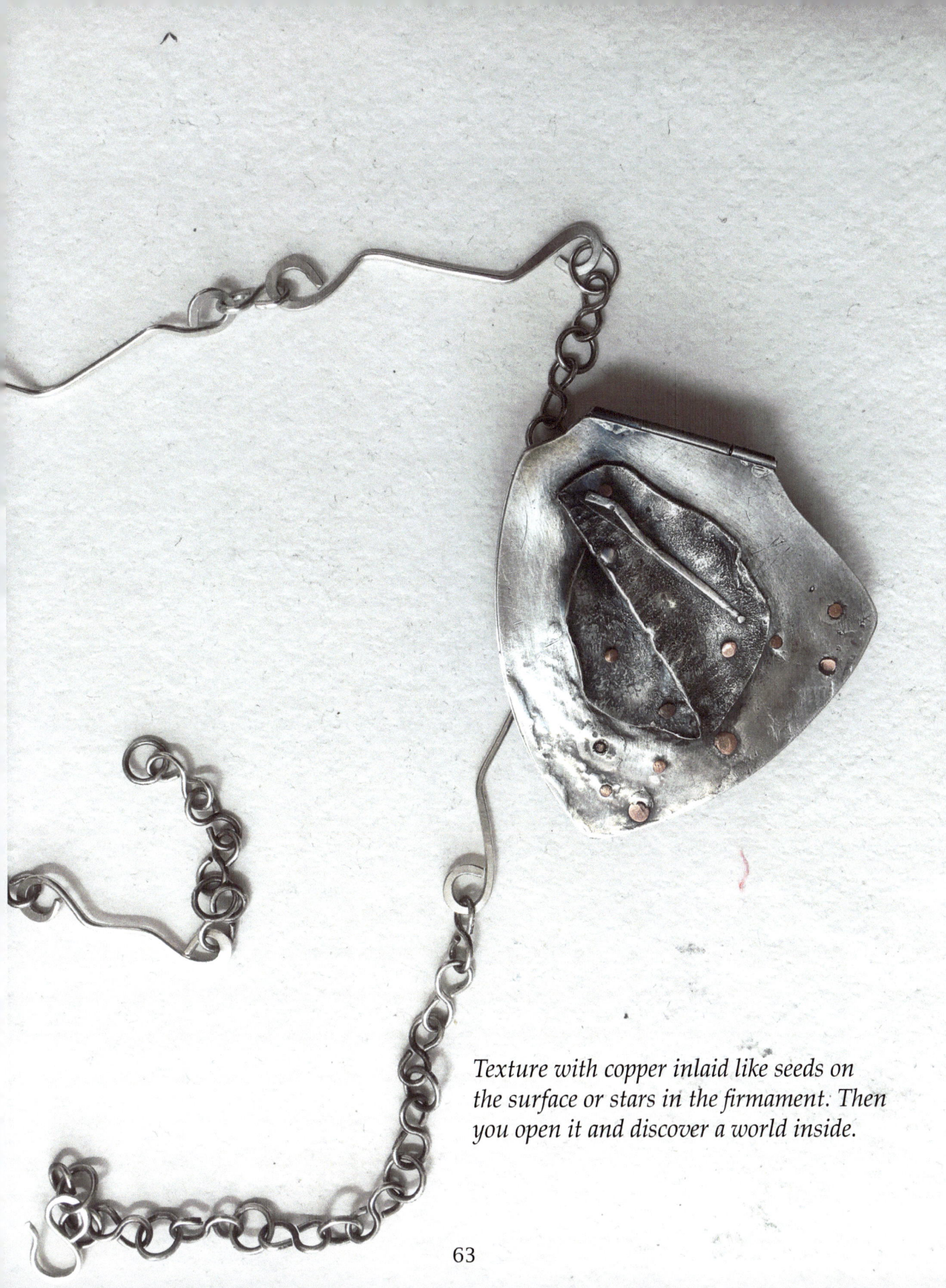

Texture with copper inlaid like seeds on the surface or stars in the firmament. Then you open it and discover a world inside.

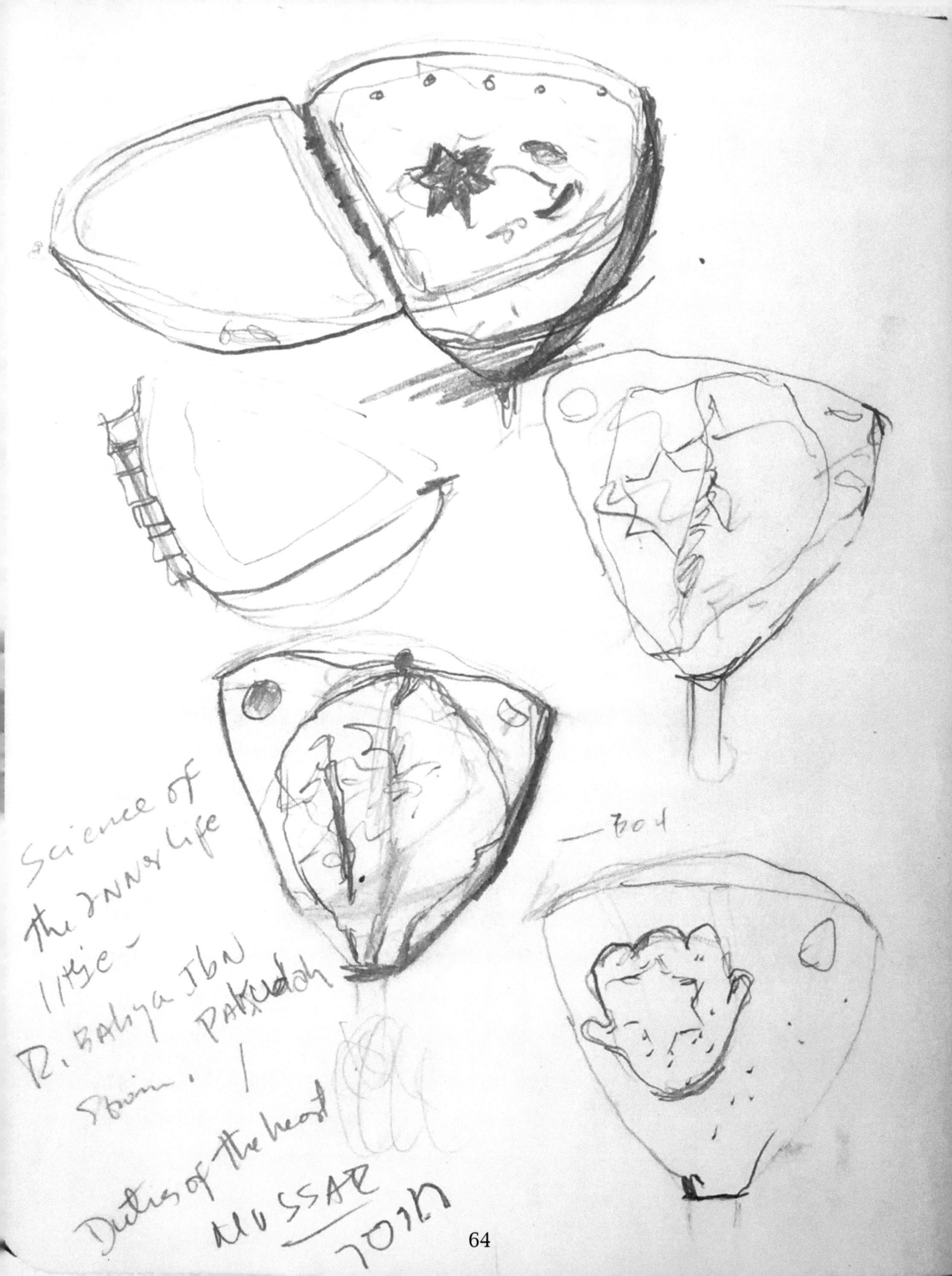

cut inside rims.

George Herbert
of 17C

reticulation :-
- anneal + air cool
- warm area - preheat block.
- place solder + lightly heat - move
pickle -

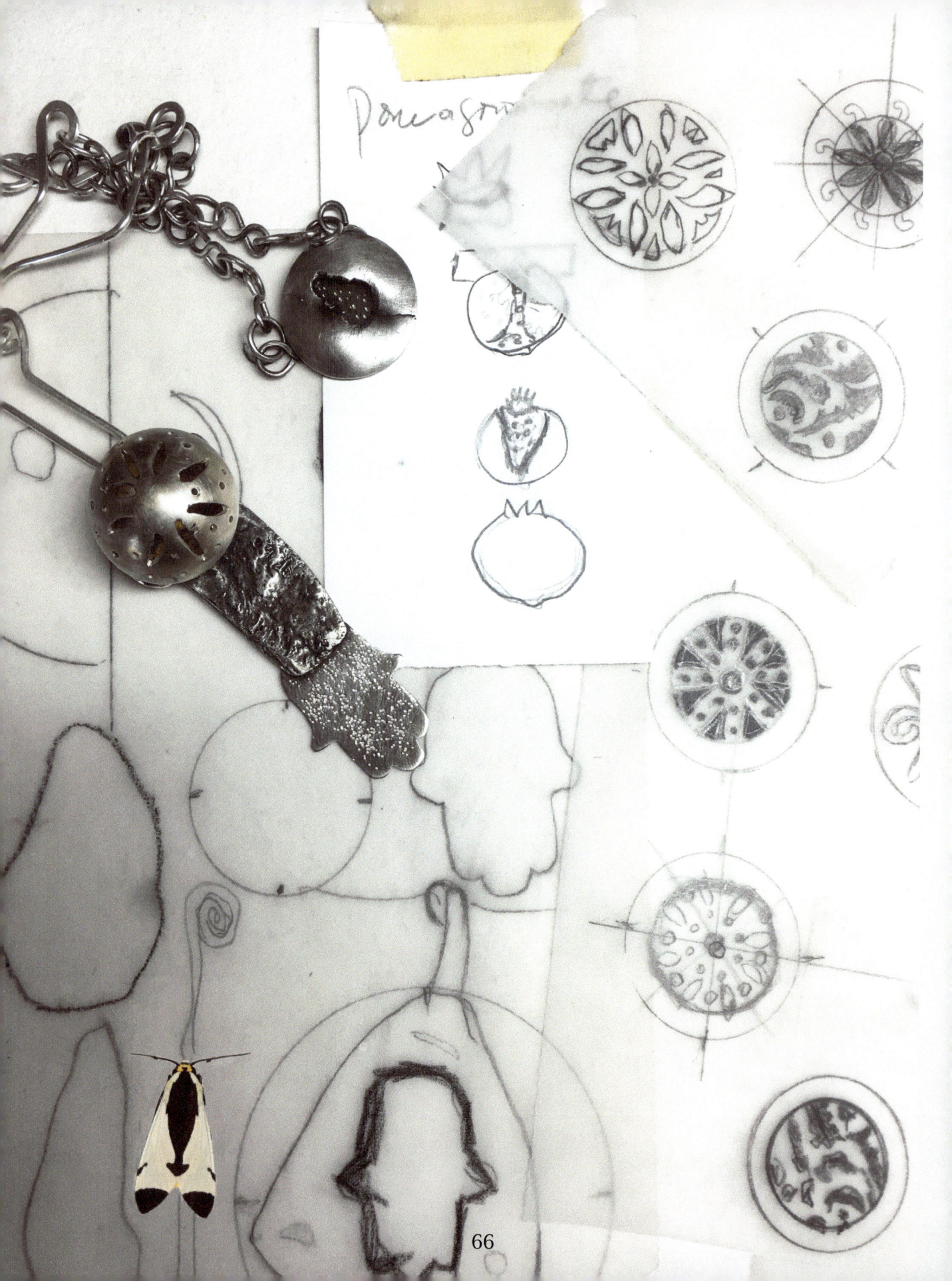

Primo Levi — the truce —
Science contributions —

___

coloring books — Mystery
nature — flowers, loops
doors, Boxes —

relaxing, therapy for mind +
Body
"escape to a world of
inspiration and artistic
fulfillment"
coloring — releases tension

new pages animals,
insects — butterflies
gardens — flowers etc

película de Greenaway —
the pillow book.

Madrid 14

Art serves to negotiate issues of identity, class, and gender, not only for marginalized groups but also for elites. Art is the product of the times, the interests people have can be seeing in the art people do —

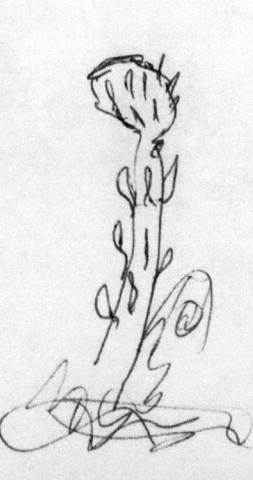

philosophy gives ideas, deep ideas to tackle life events. How do we process what we see? How to put out the expression of the impact of what we see or hear?

one piece

1,896 -
notissimo judi
en sevilla

I do art for myself, for my senses — I just put ideas together and develop what I see could work. I like to combine elements either color, shapes

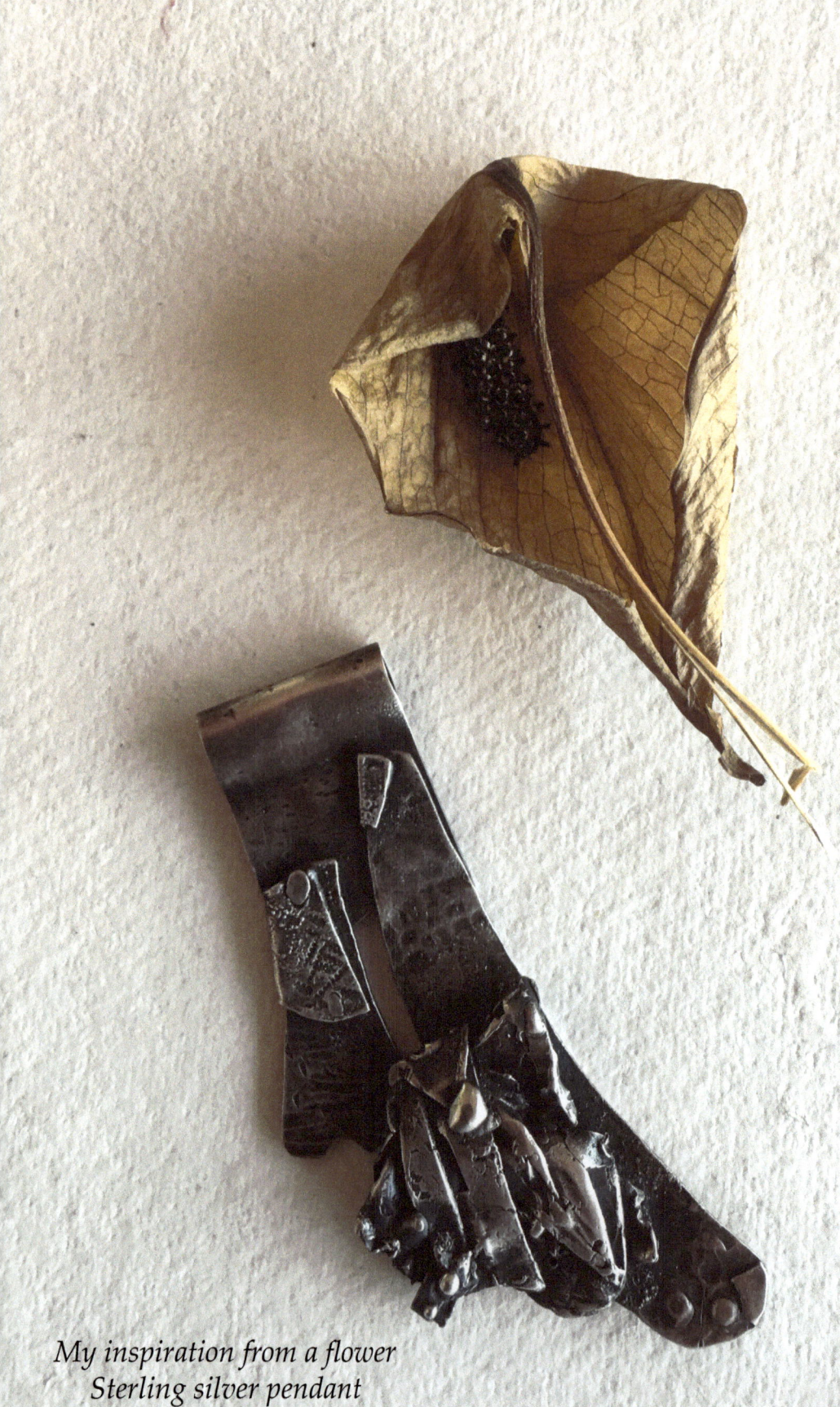

My inspiration from a flower
Sterling silver pendant

Jacques Derrida – "Felt the other" as Jew in North Africa

Deconstruction – debunking the established tradition.

confusion + doubt are not to be embarrassed about

deconstruction of political systems, institutions, TRADITION

post-modern philosophy –

Language is subjective since every individual has an understanding of meaning —

Skepticism of modernism –

Politics of authenticity

We all are interested in knowing the meaning of what we observe and live. But, it is all subjective. Who are you, where and when is the observer

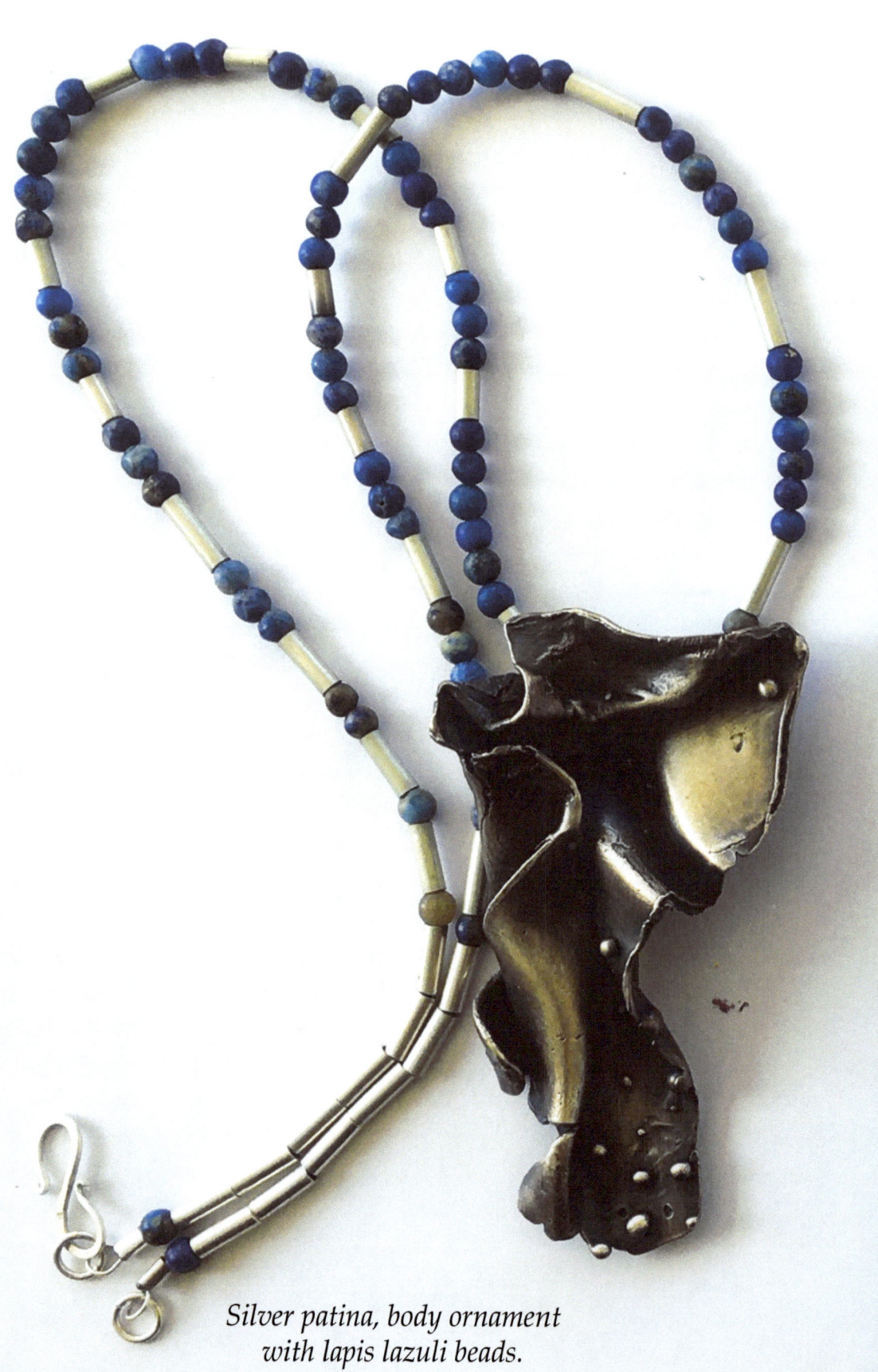

Silver patina, body ornament with lapis lazuli beads.

Looking at nature constantly makes my life poetic. I look at the folds and lines that a simple dried flower gives us to admire, this is my source of inspiration in my seasons & years. Although Nature has always been my Muse, now more than ever I look more carefully.

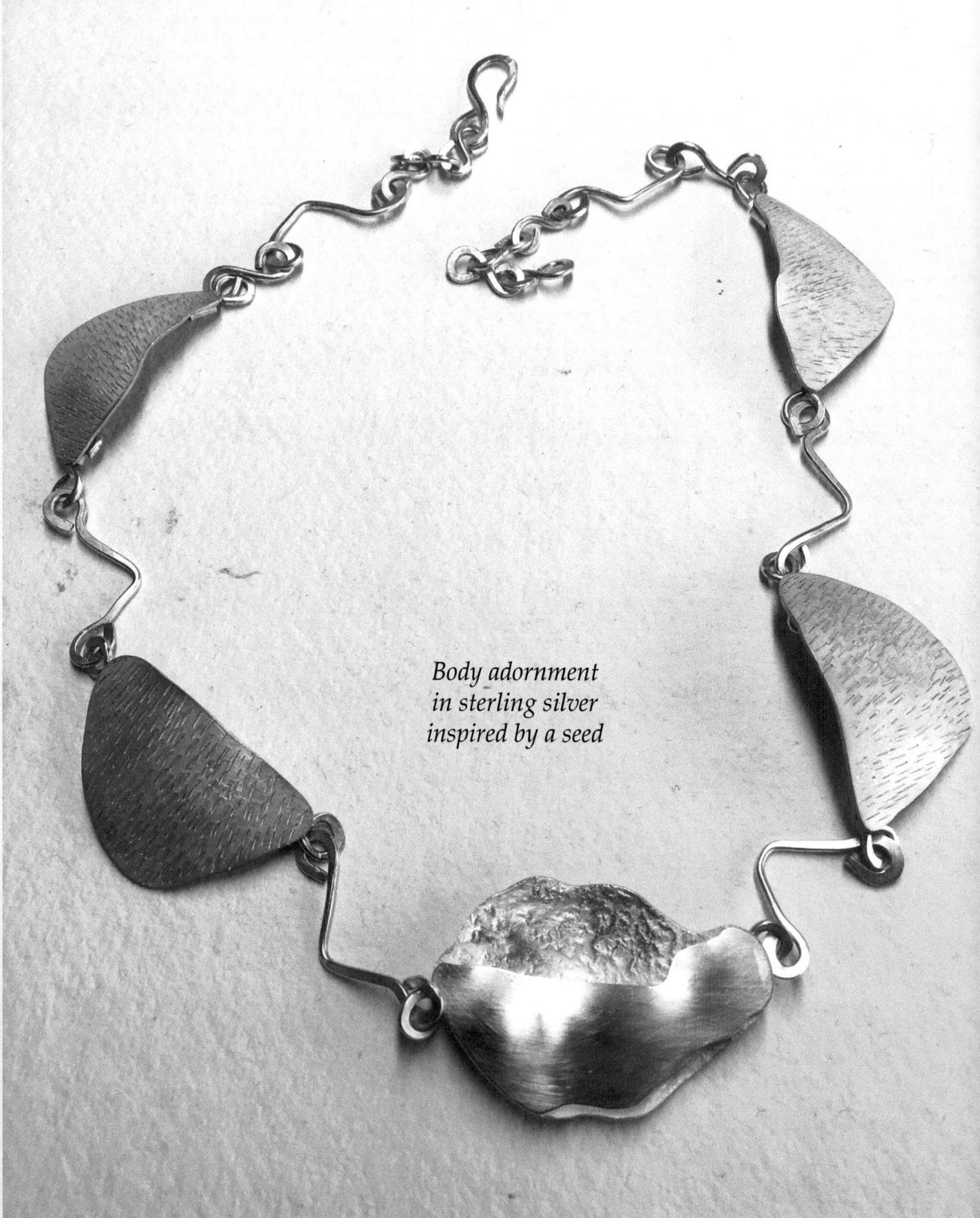

Body adornment in sterling silver inspired by a seed

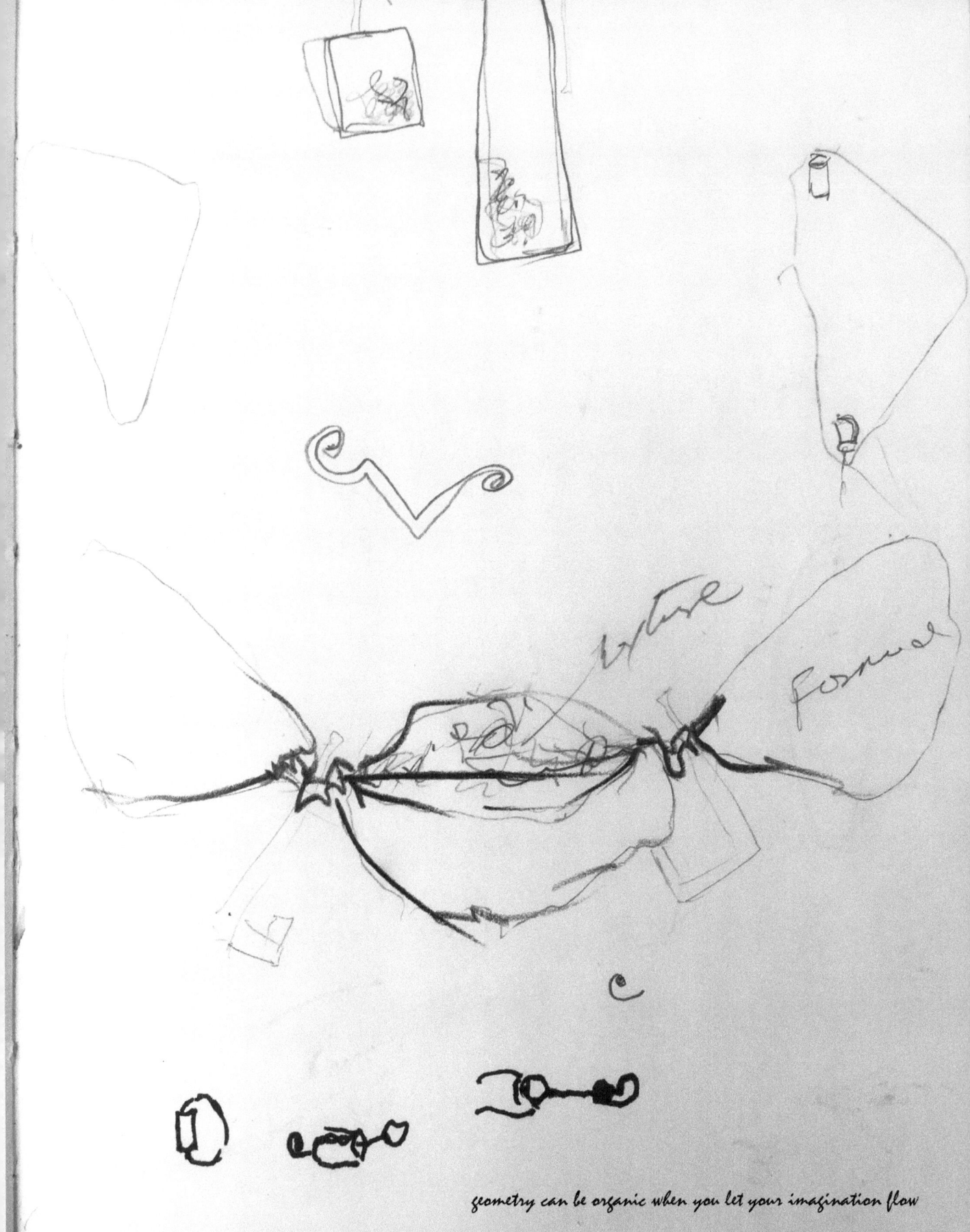

geometry can be organic when you let your imagination flow

So many lives, so many things to do, to think, to accomplish — It's a reverie — un placer, tener la expansión temporal para desarrollar Hoy q' usar tus intuición, ser rápida en tus acción y no tener miedo.

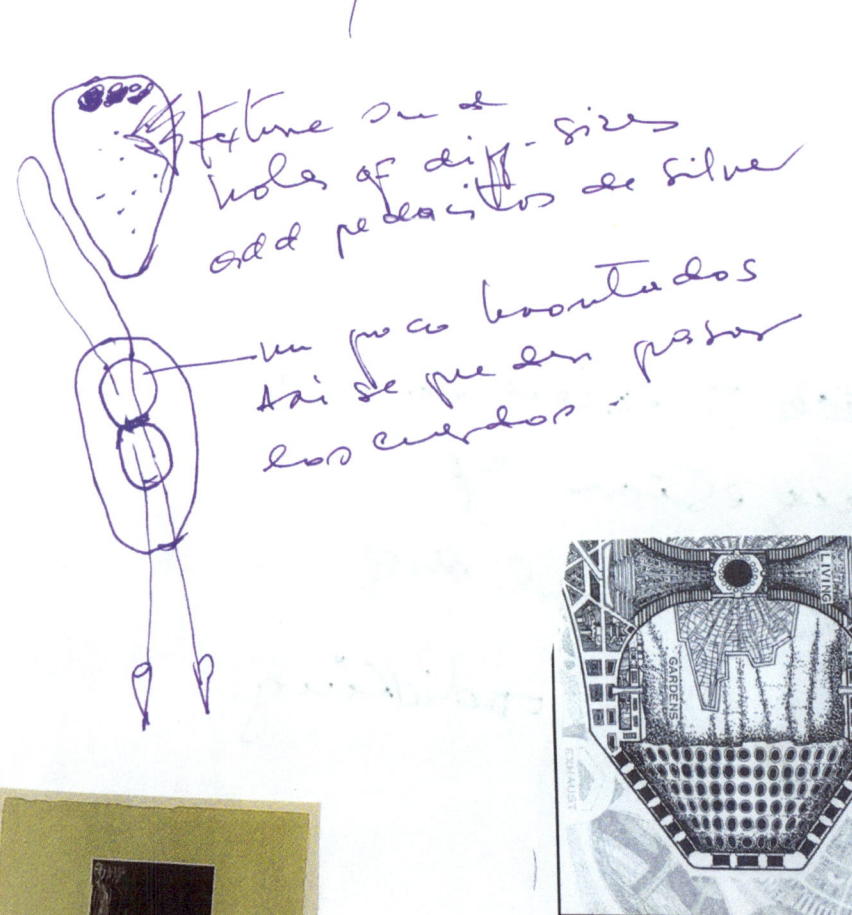

texture on it
holes of diff. sizes
add pedacitos de silver

un poco levantados
así se pueden pasar
los cuerdos

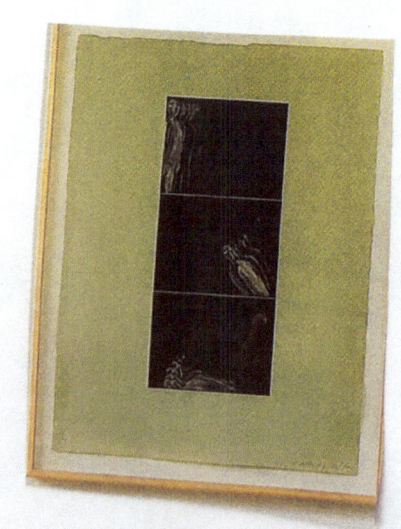

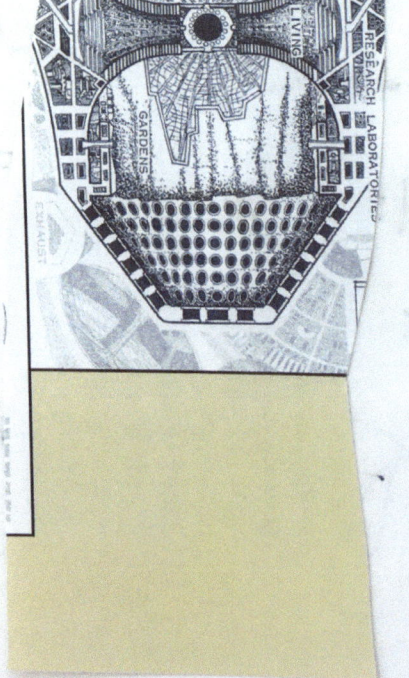

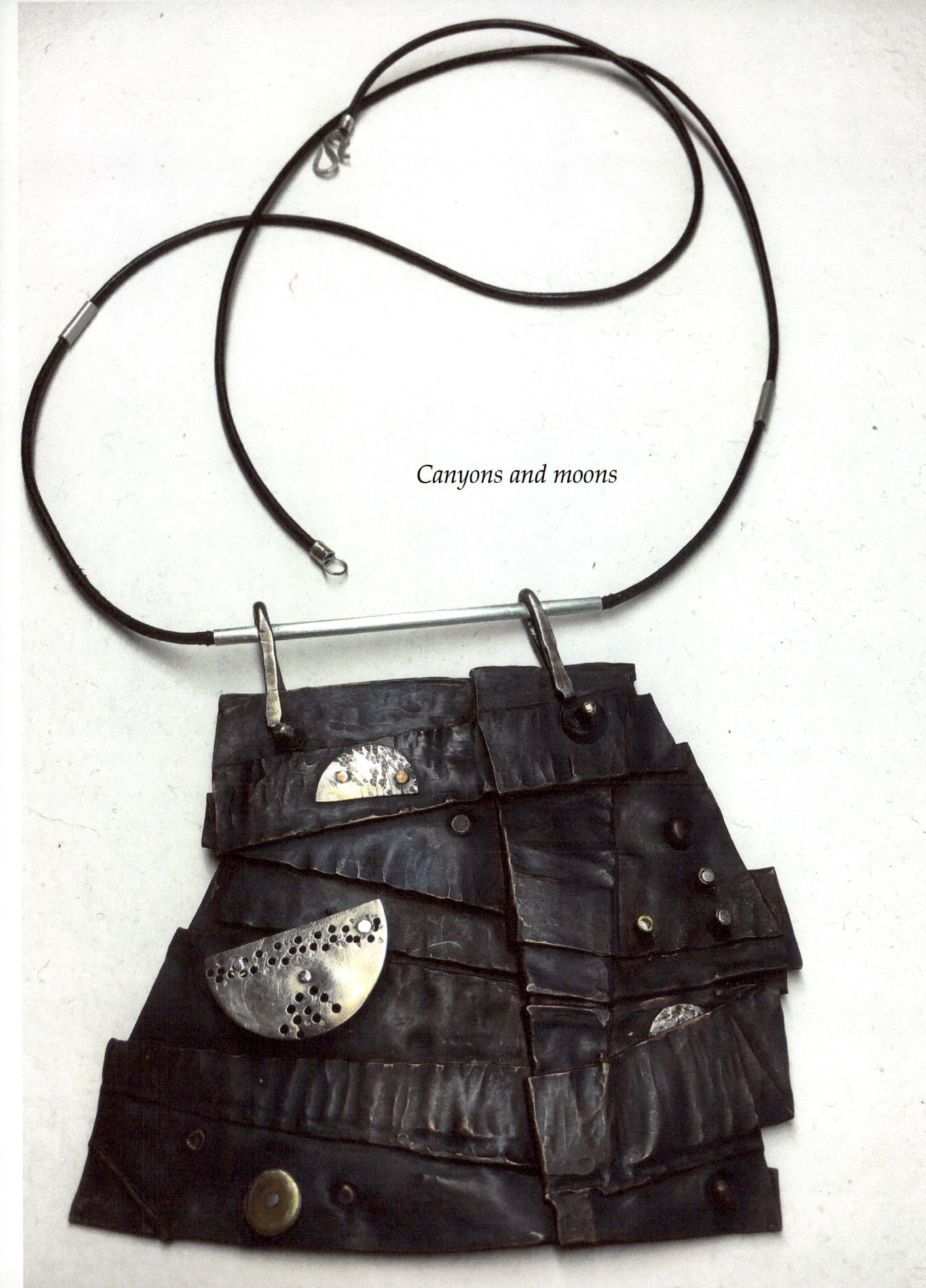
Canyons and moons

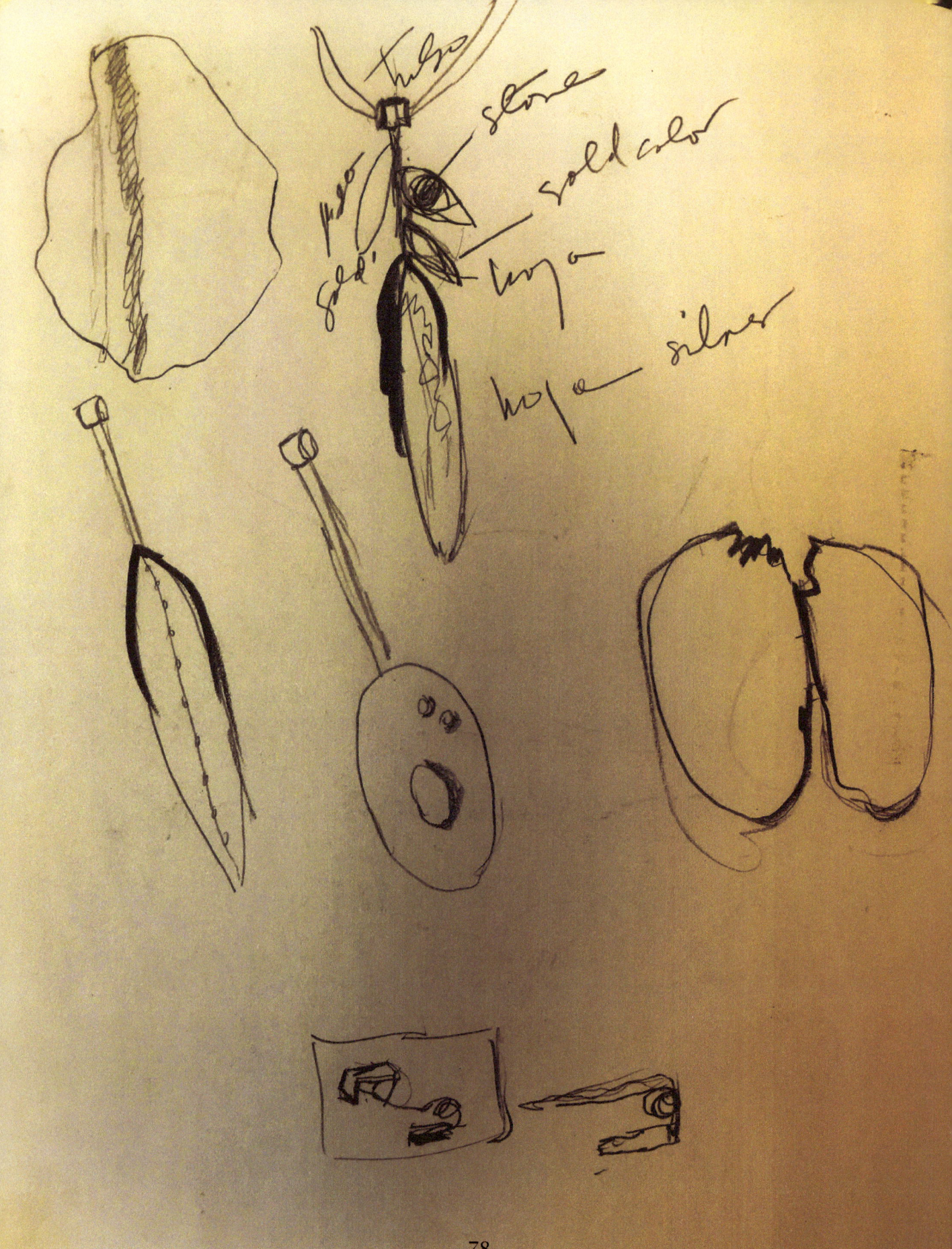

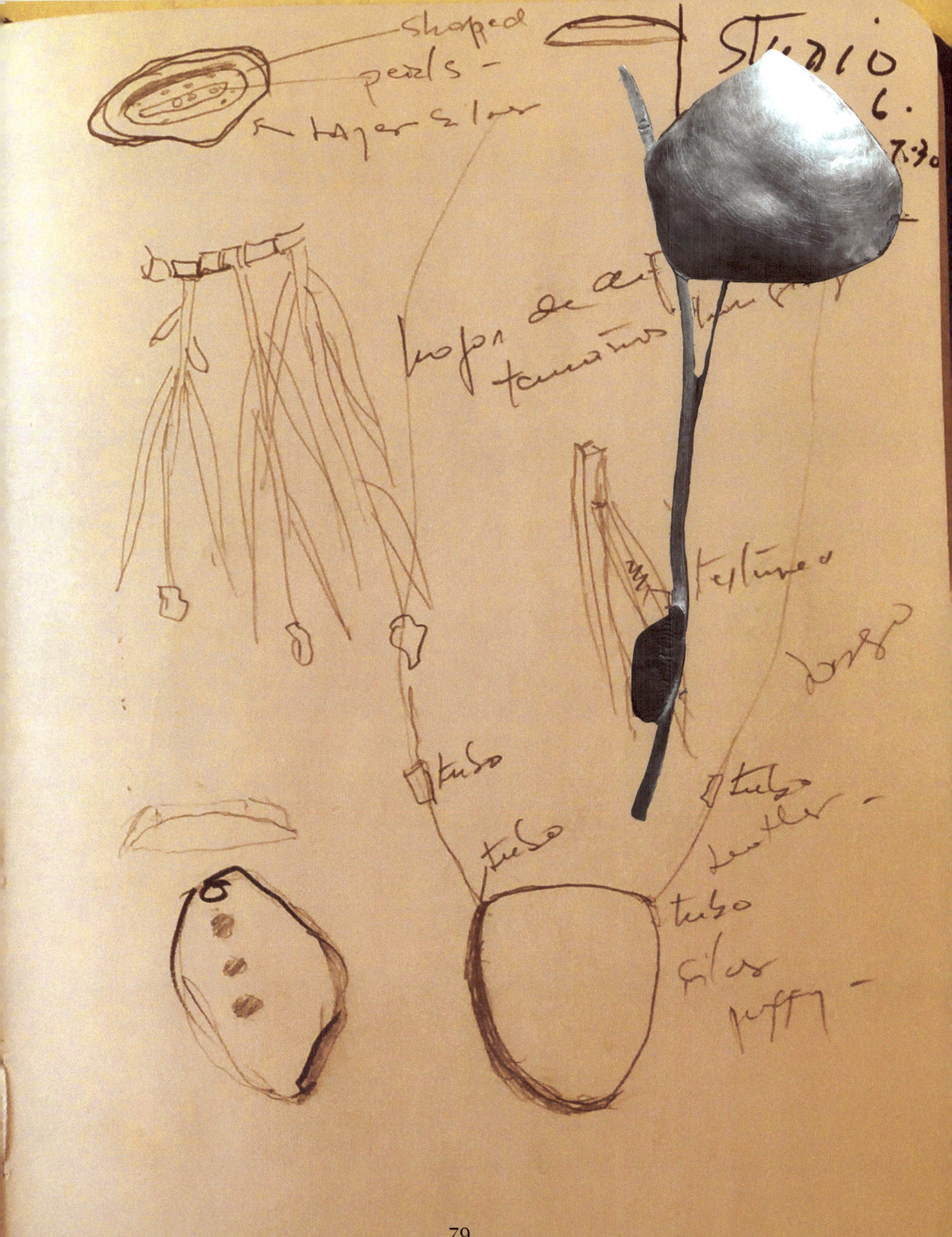

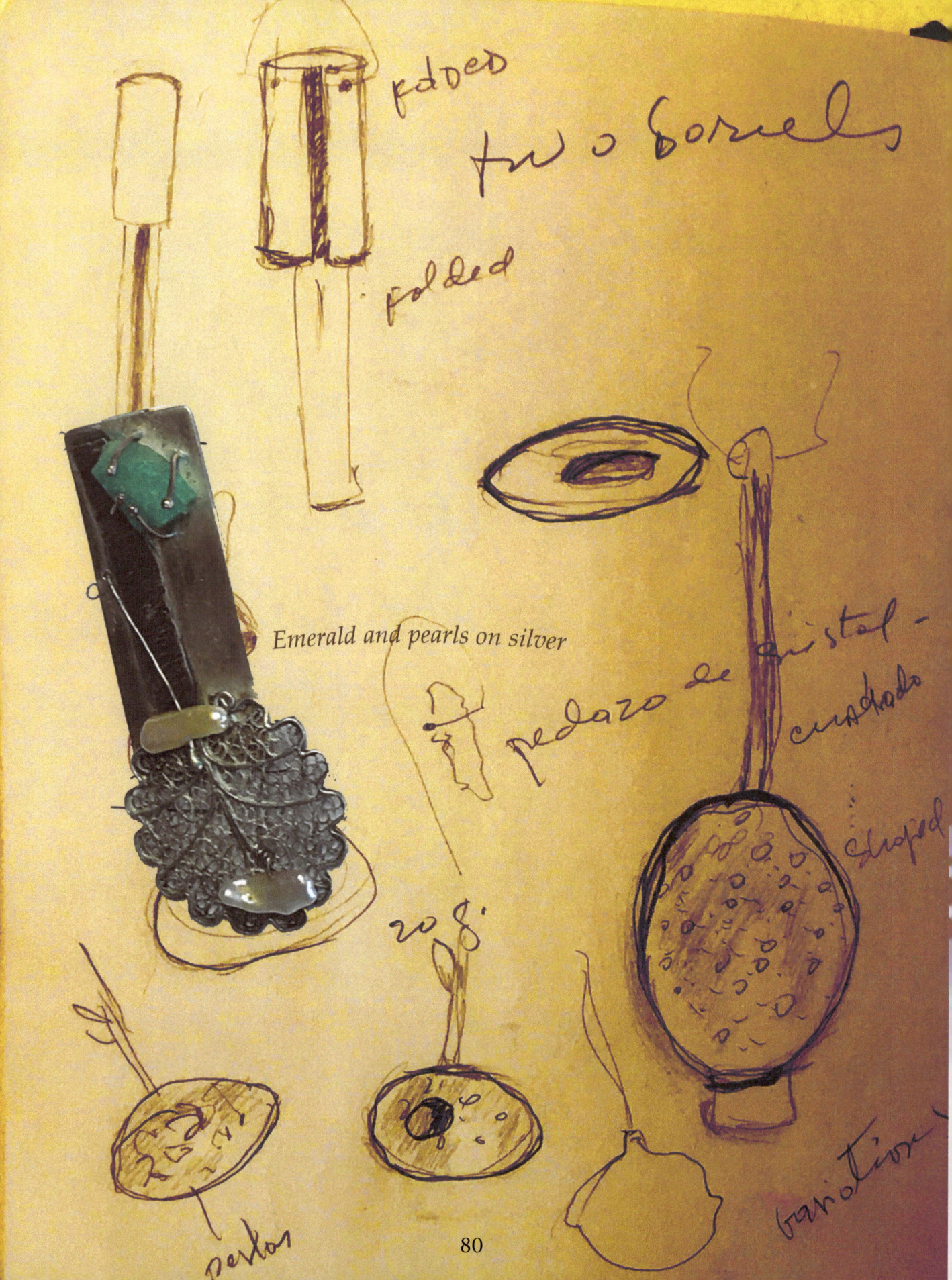

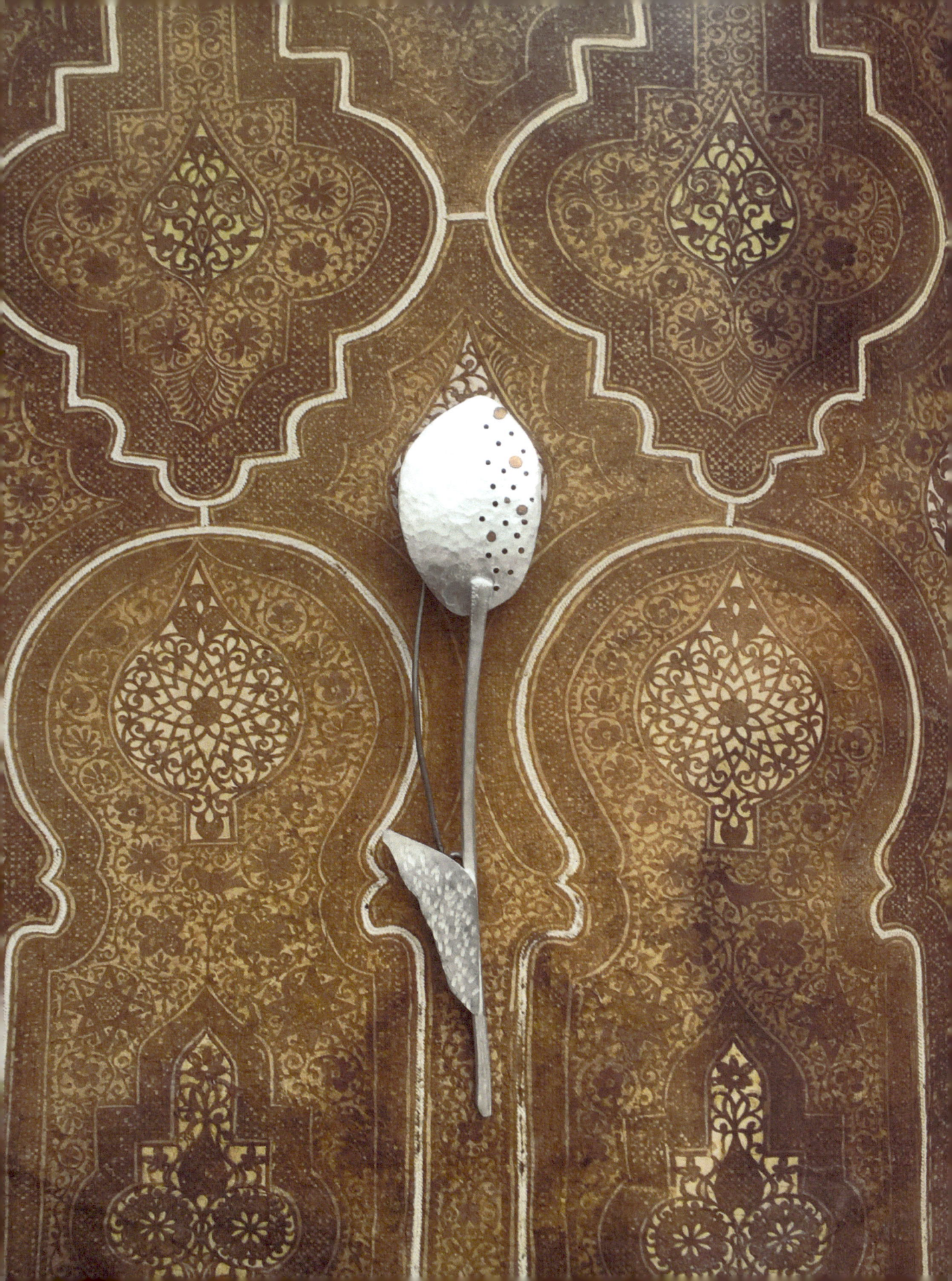

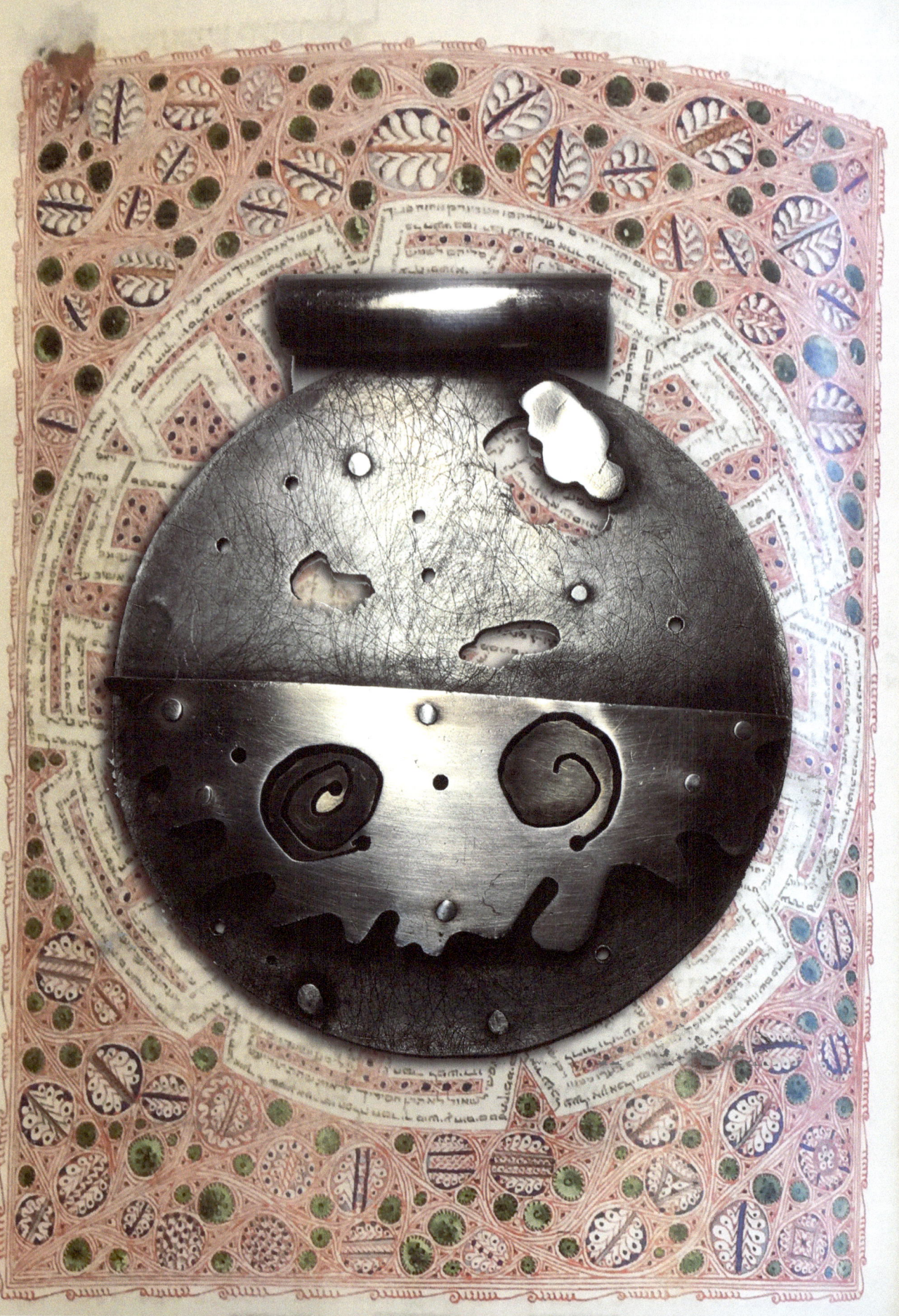

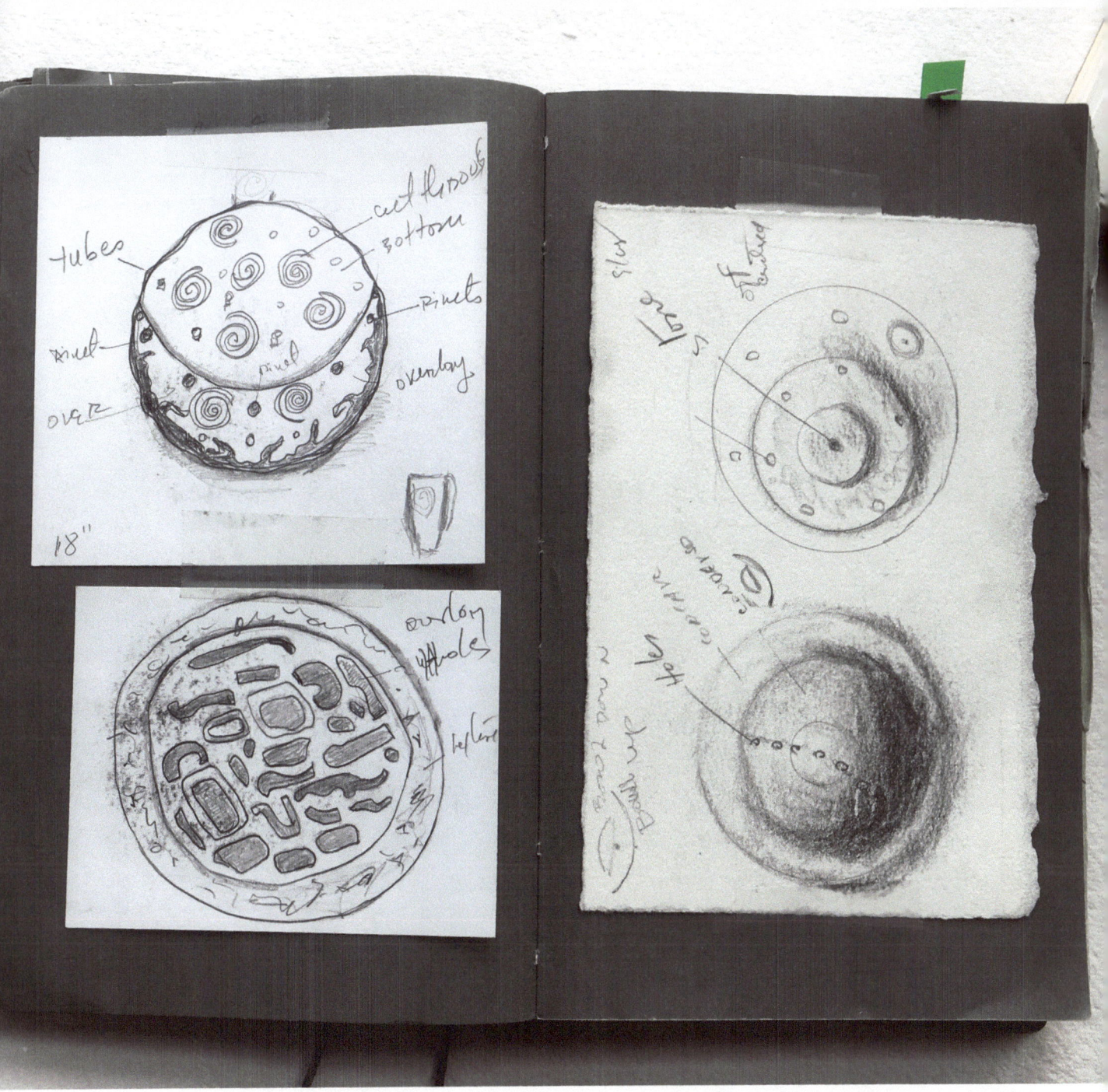

Straight lines that curve and make clouds and spirals, negative spaces, dots that dance on the surface like stars in the firmament. Inspired by a carpet page from the Medieval Spanish Hebrew Bible from La Coruña. (Kennicott Bible at the Bodleian Library Oxford)

I like positive and negative spaces, relief, light, shadows, and textured surfaces.

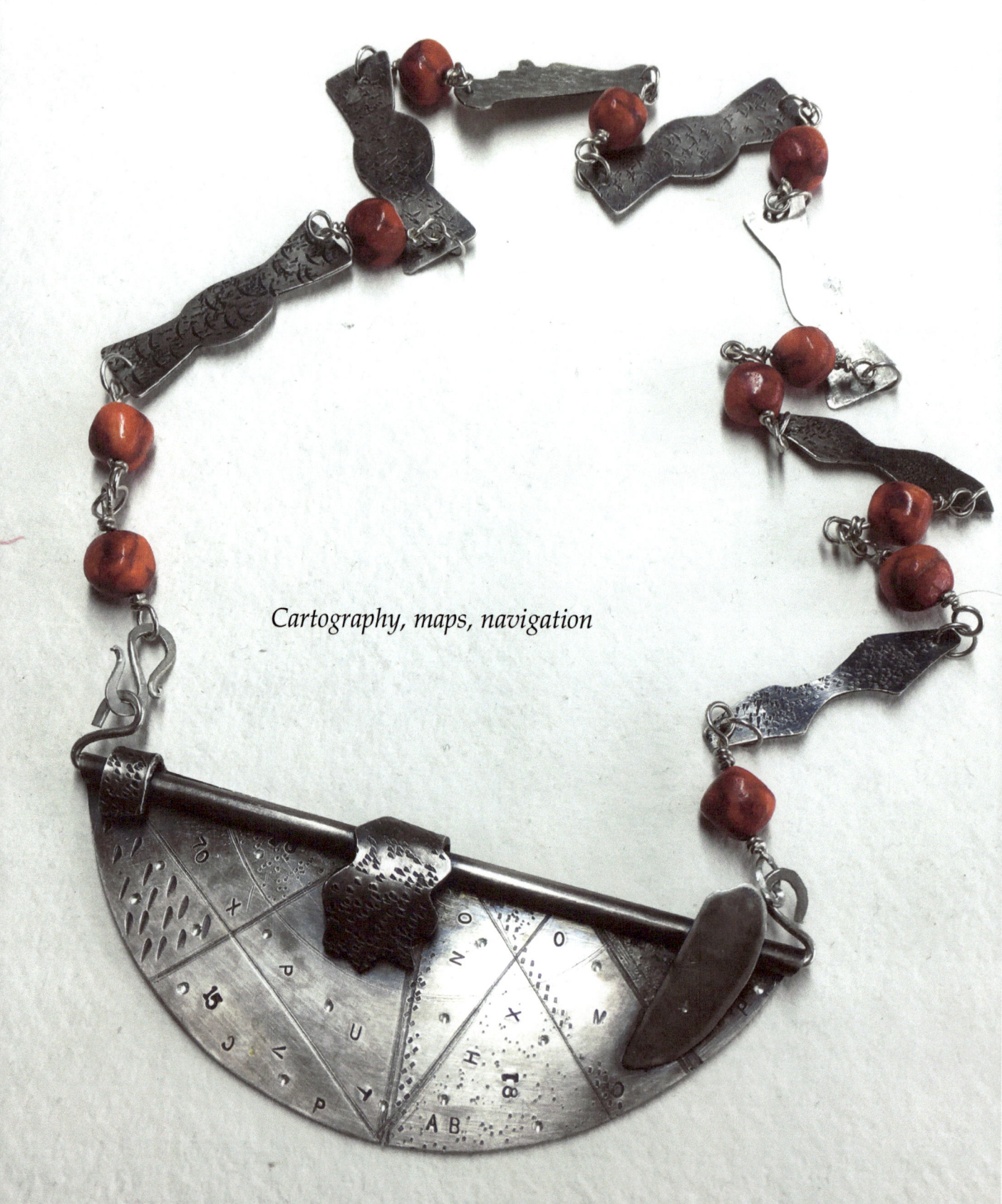

Cartography, maps, navigation

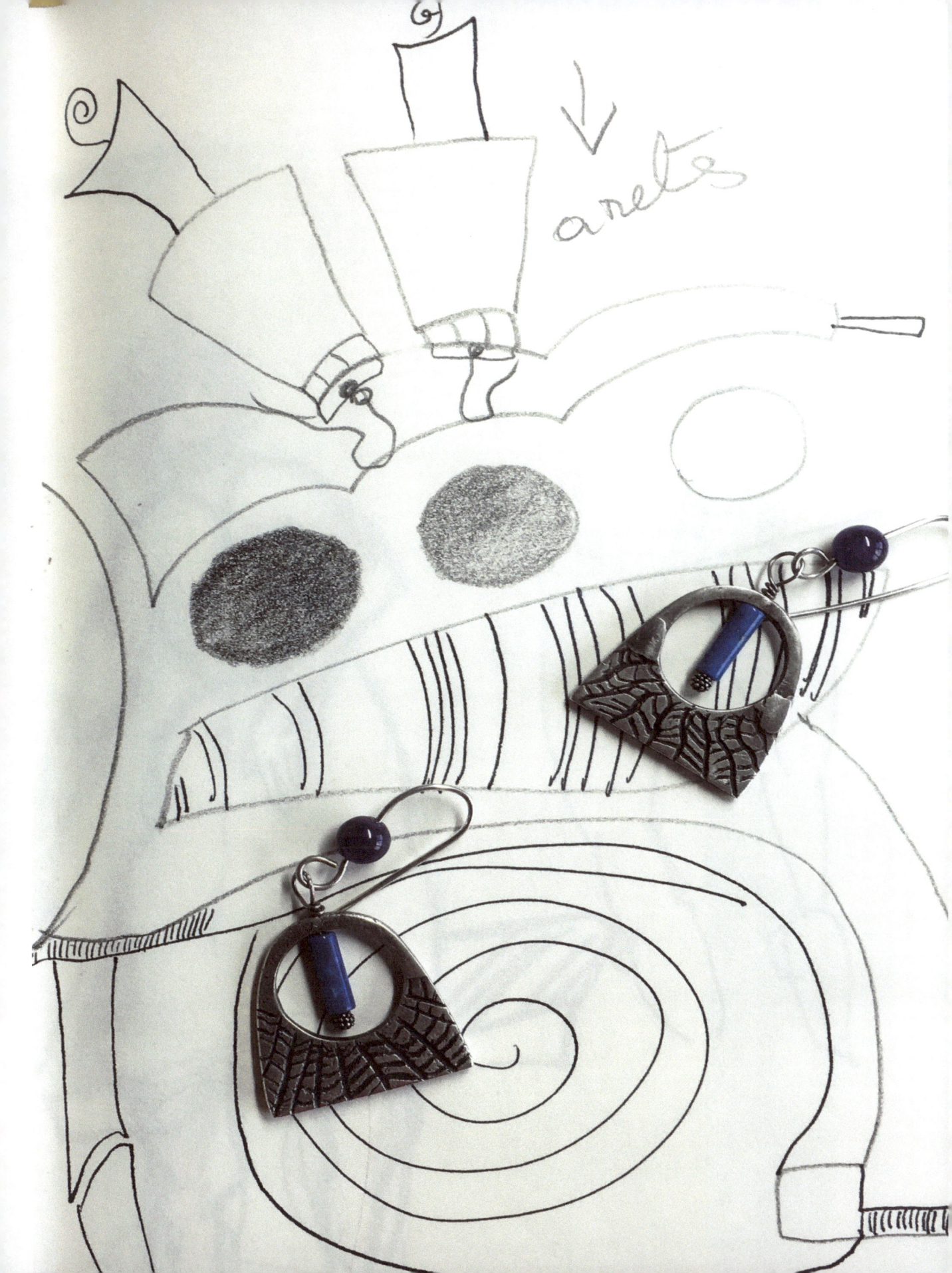

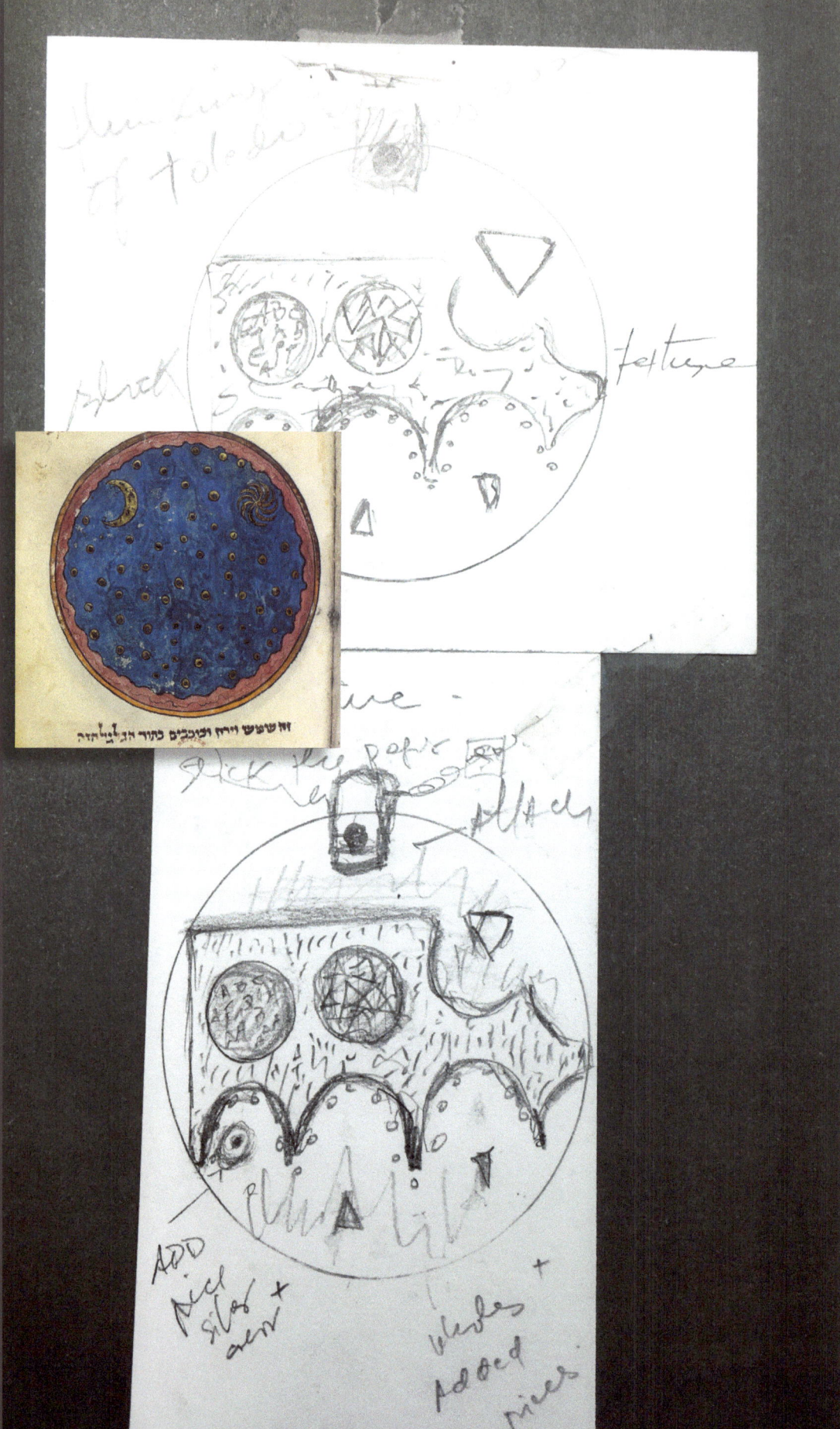

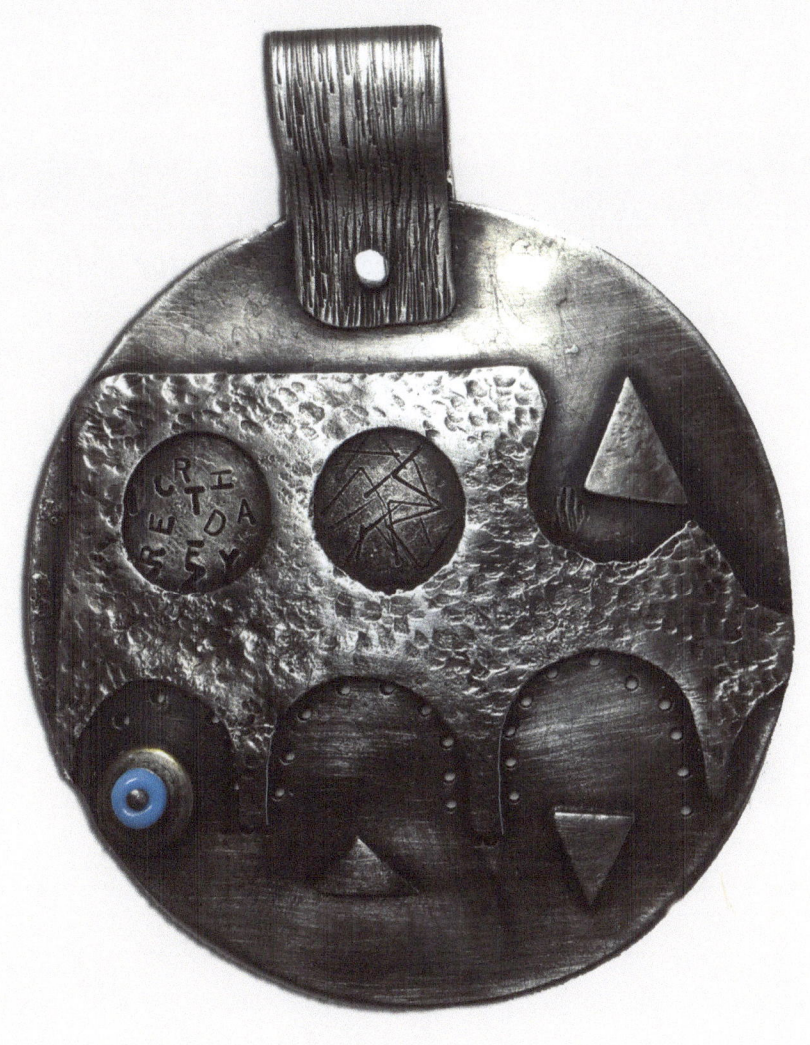

I like the idea of a line that makes circles and arches.
Inspired by Toledo the walled ancient city with its history of
Jews, Muslims and Christians, its medieval arches and huge
doors to protect the community at night.

I treat silver graphically with lines, texture, relief,
and patina to give a piece the strength of age.

Leaves that go from the garden to my head.
From organic to idea in silver to adorn the body.

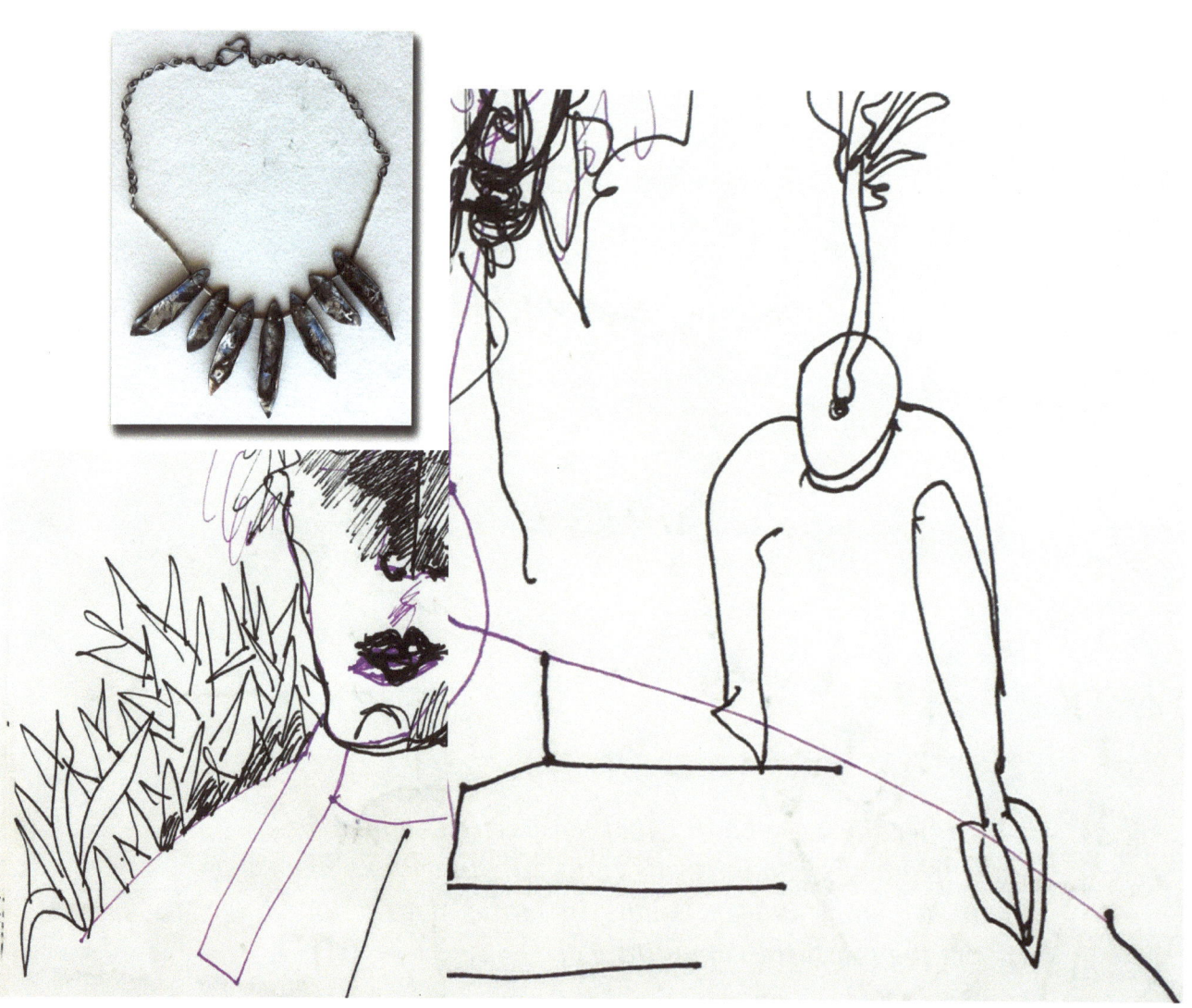

sterling silver, wood, bone
pieces of chain

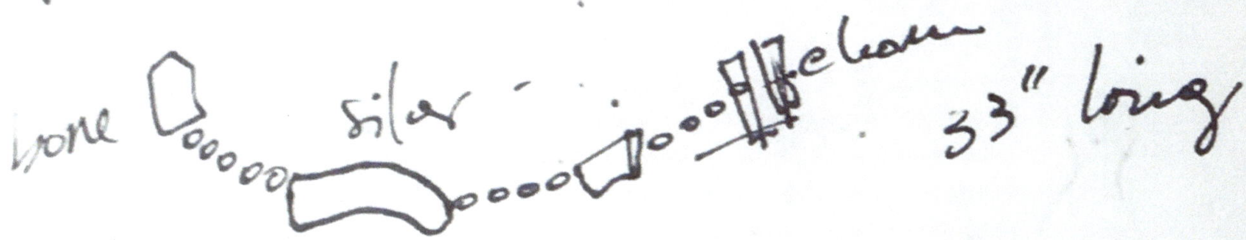

bone — silver — chain   33" long

---

sterling silver, objects - carnelian beads
washers - size chain.

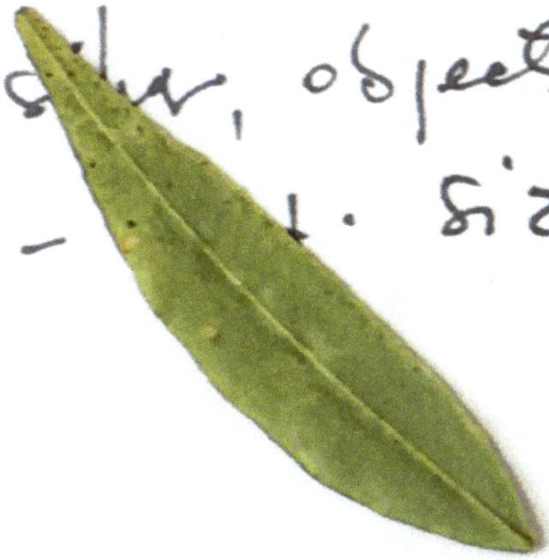

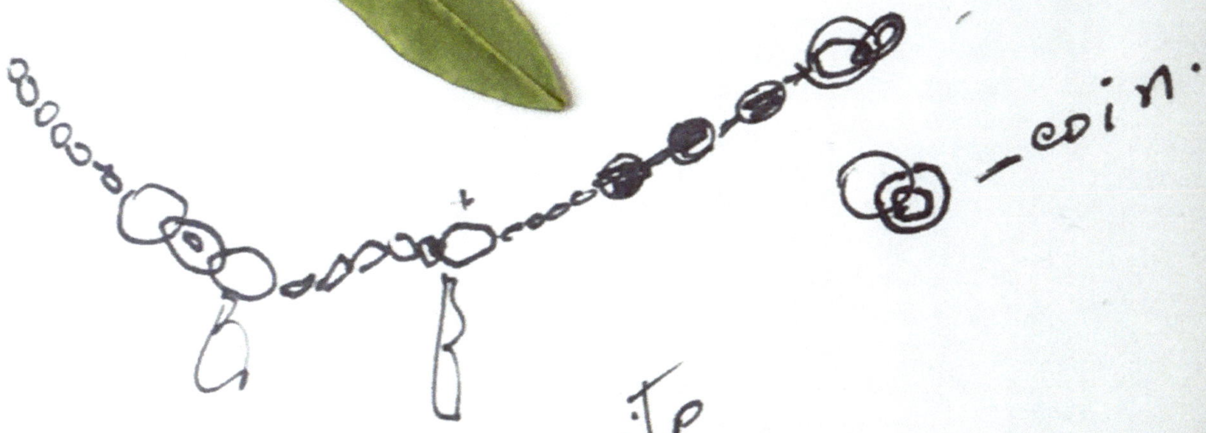

— coin.

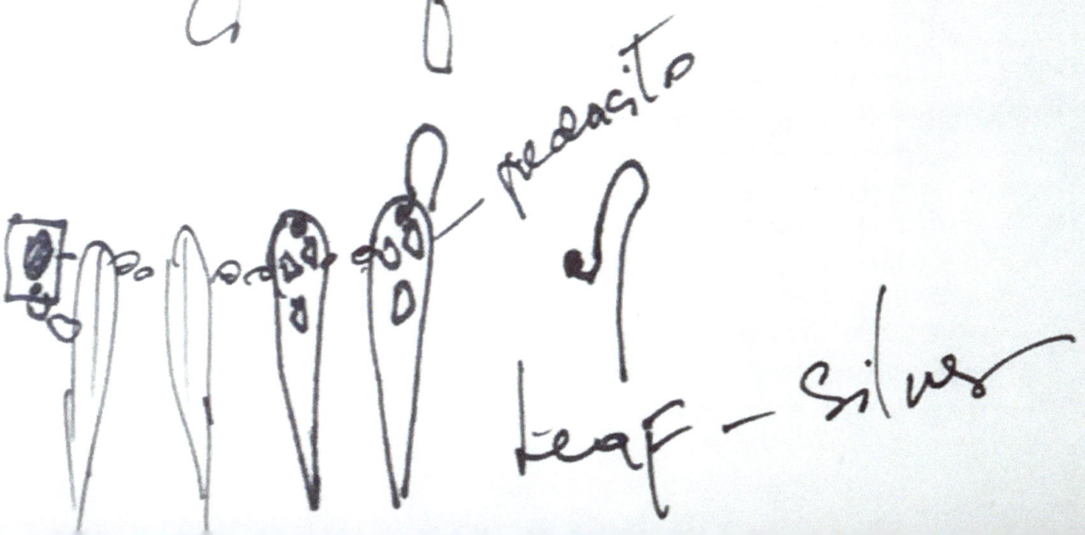

pedacito

leaf — silver

Londres taxis LONDON

44 1223 715715. Fun this taxi

MATI — PND bus —
          bus —
miercols — 10 P.M.   io —

NEVERA —

Bus — National Express —
COACH
Ase —   — 13 guineas
to Cambridge — UK.

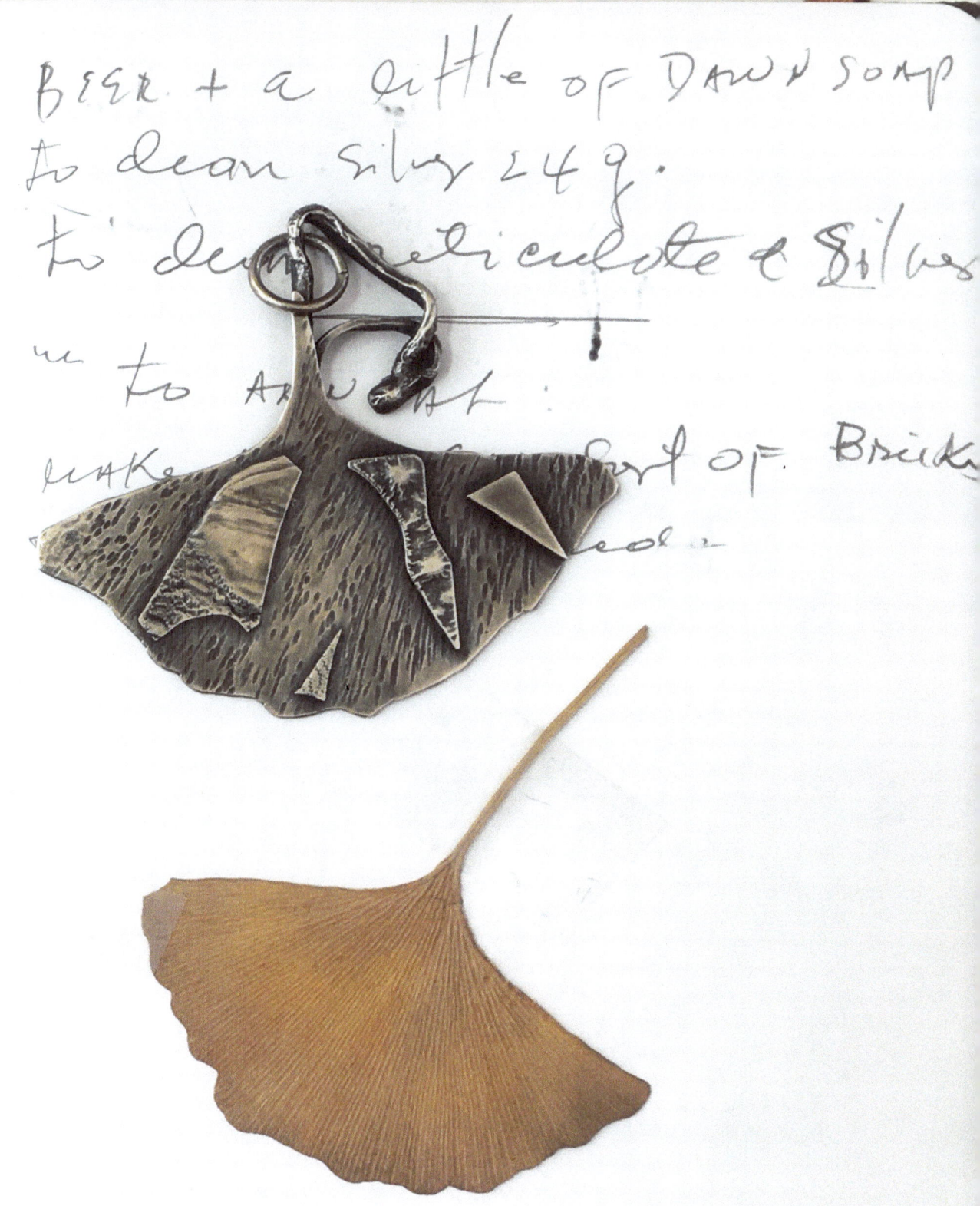

My response to a fallen leaf

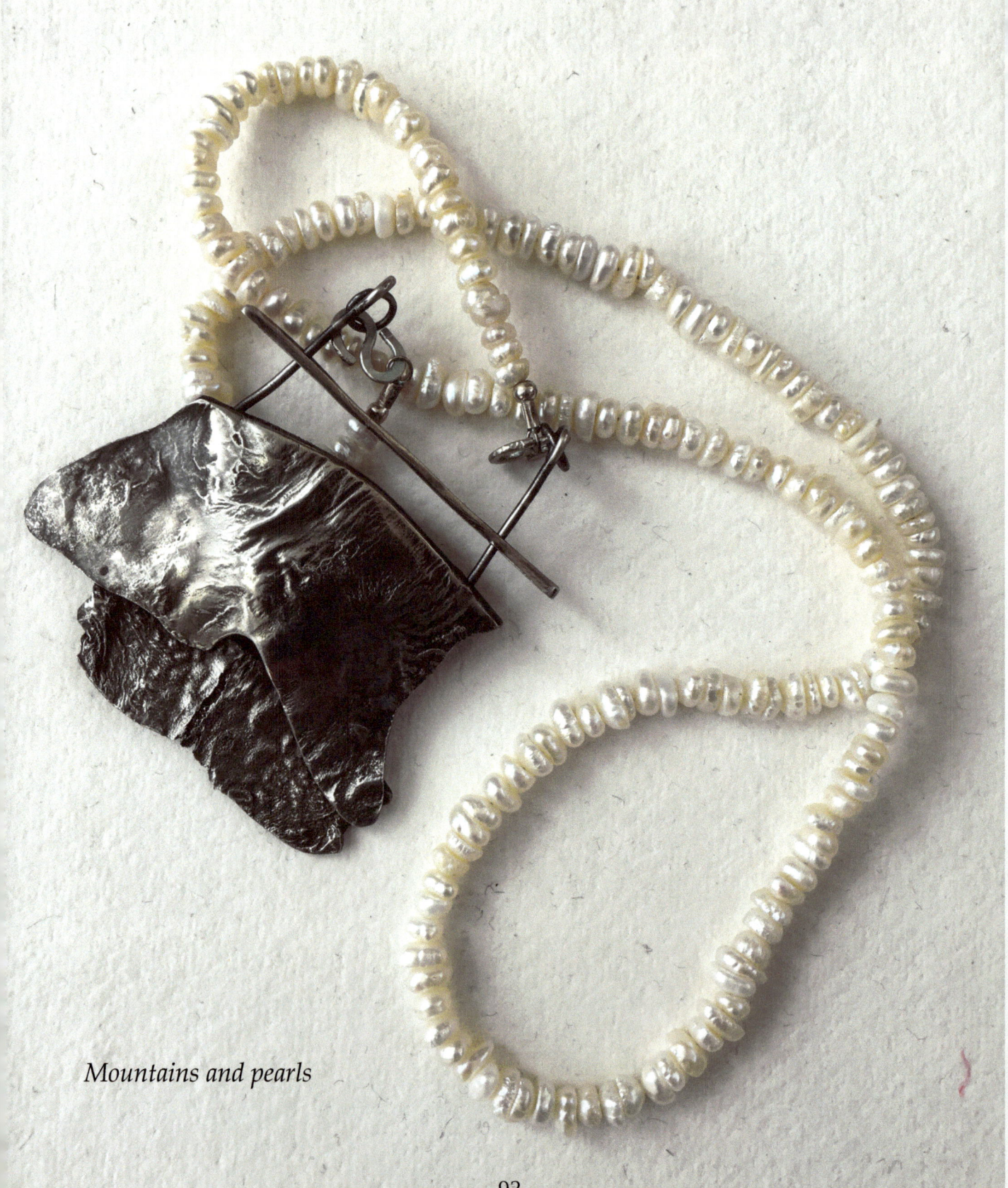
Mountains and pearls

Creativity is a gift that everyone has. It depends how you develop it.

Imagination and problem solving are results of creativity the creative person solves problems in an imaginative way very personal.

Transformation is the essence of ~~doing~~ creative art.

Art is not defined by technique not by copying exactly what you see —

turn things around, add elements that are disparate, enlarge, compress, stretch — make something that might refer to the original.

Drawing is freedom.
When you are drawing something, generally it turns into something else. That's the difference with writing. Words have specific meaning. You can let your hand go and invent no matter where it goes.

understanding self knowledge
identity, culture

Should Kafka belong to Germany or to Jerusalem that was the question in the trials of the ownership of his papers that Brod had saved and were in dispute. Interesting that Kafka wanted to burn his writings...

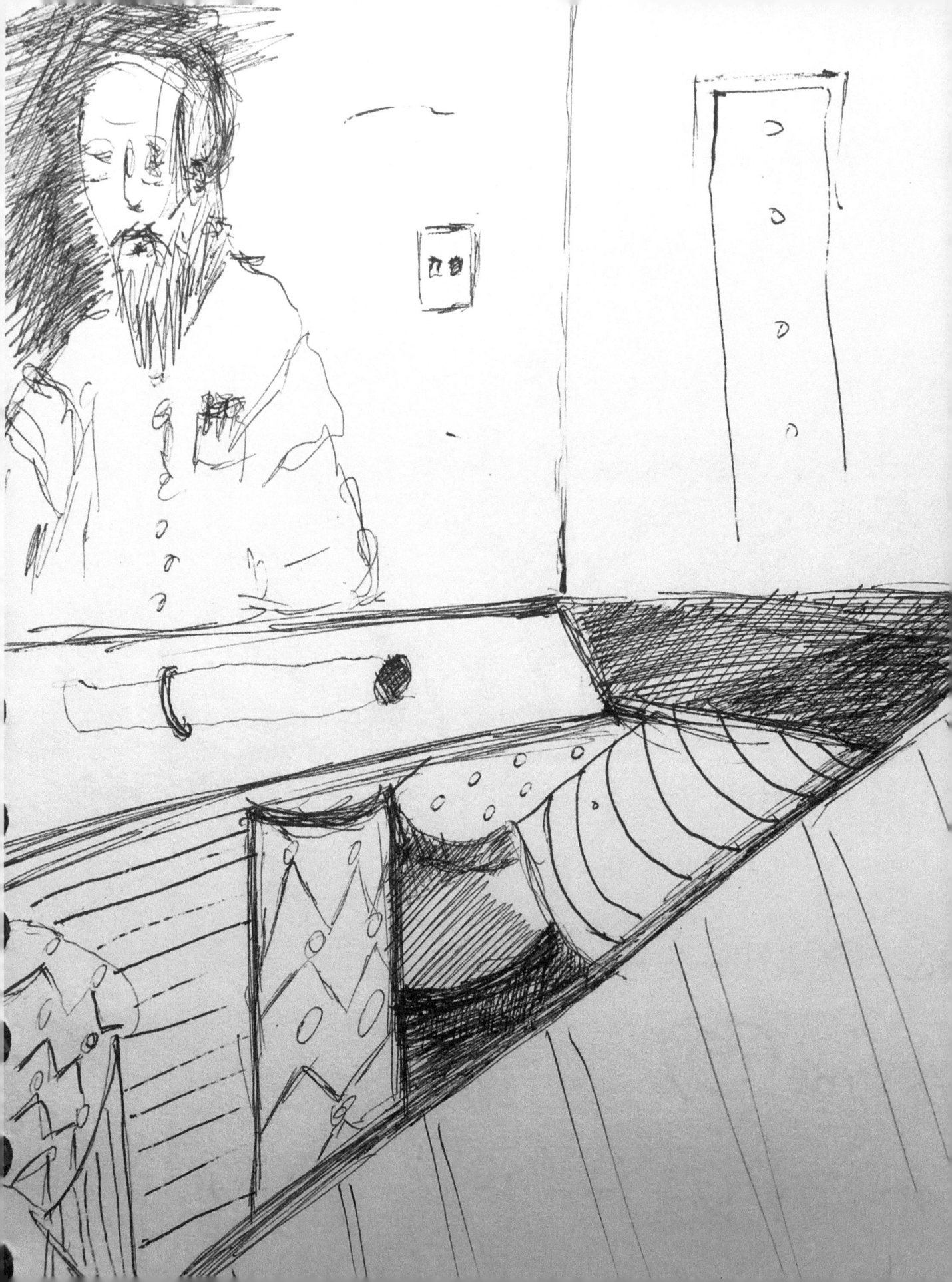

Silence is the sound of life.
In silence we create, in silence
we think and make decisions.
Silence is part of music,
Silence is expansive.

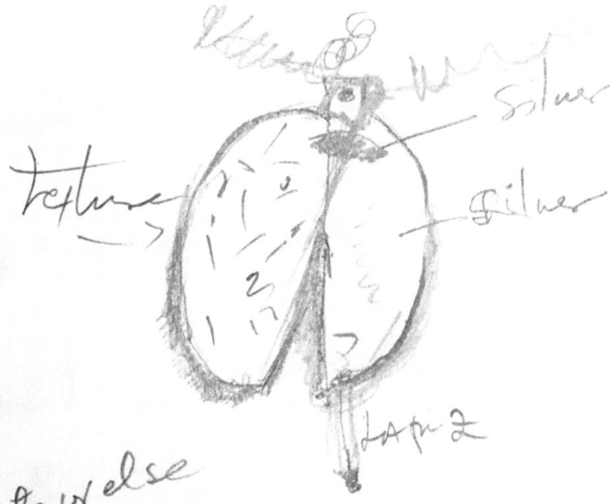

silver solder
texture
silver
lapiz

wearable works of art

Philosophy

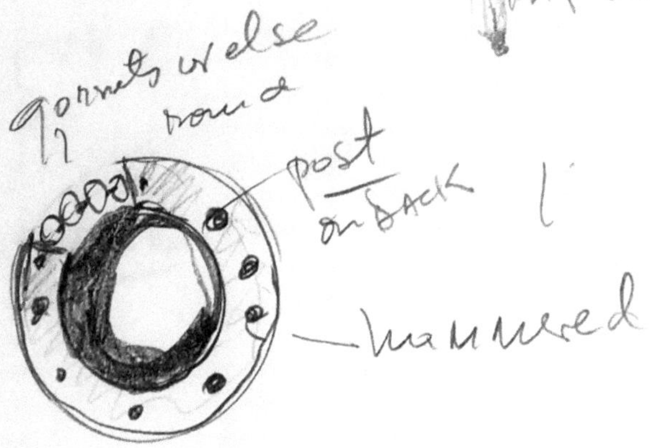

garnets or else round
post on back
hammered

Jules [illegible]
2017

the inner history of mankind is the
(essence) or history of literature -
— literature expresses a culture
HBO Elena Ferrante's
"My Brilliant Friend"

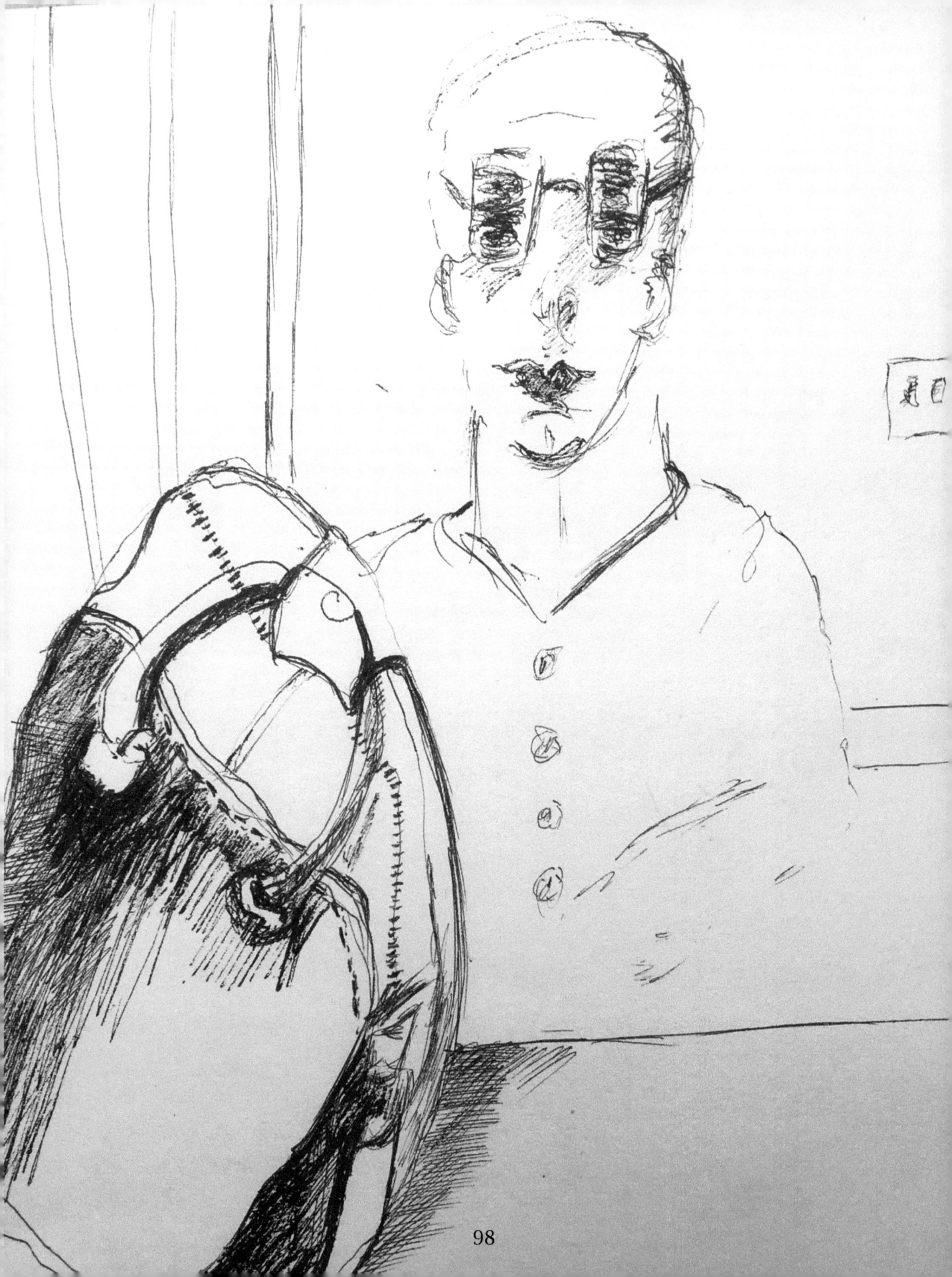

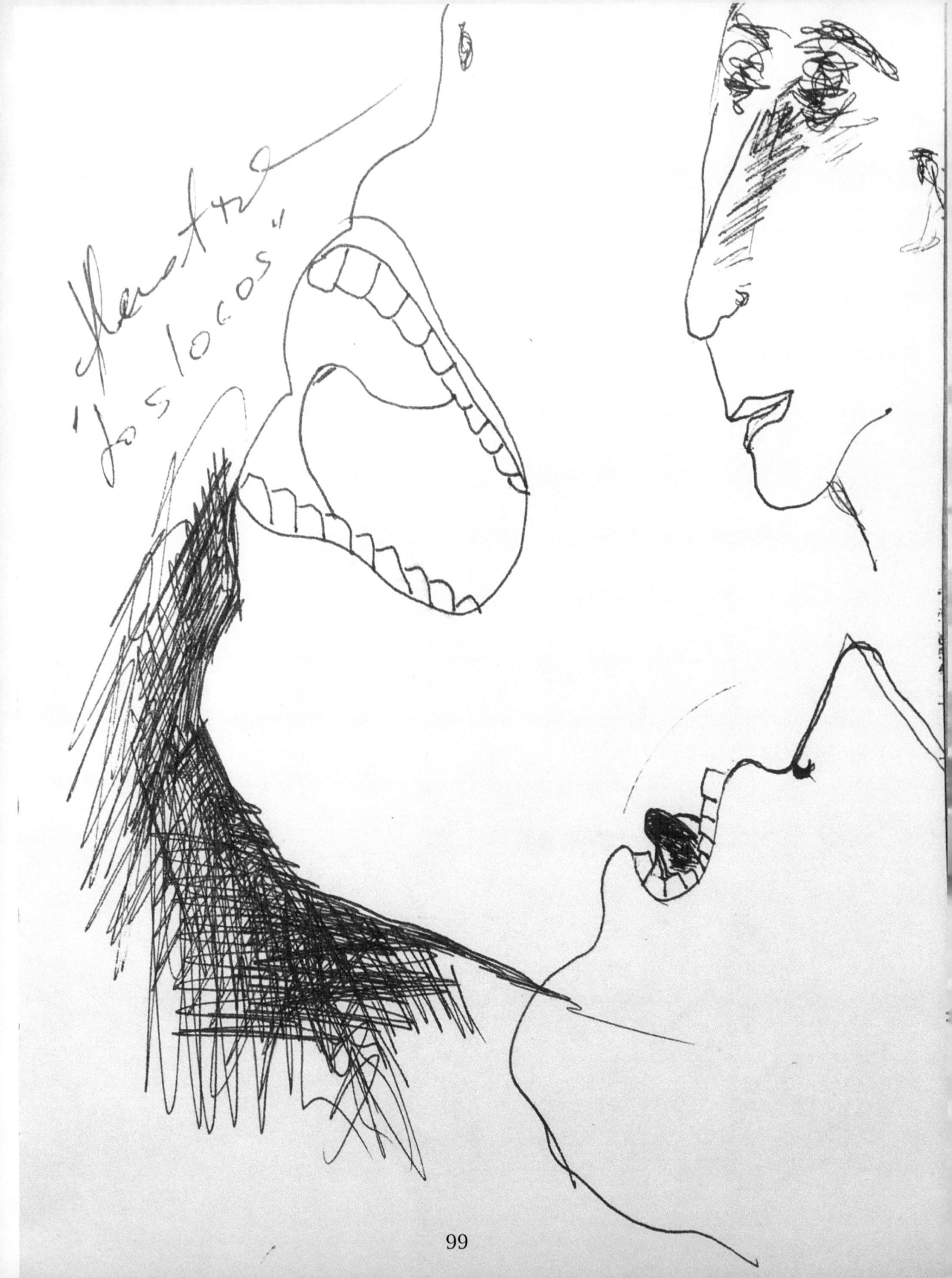

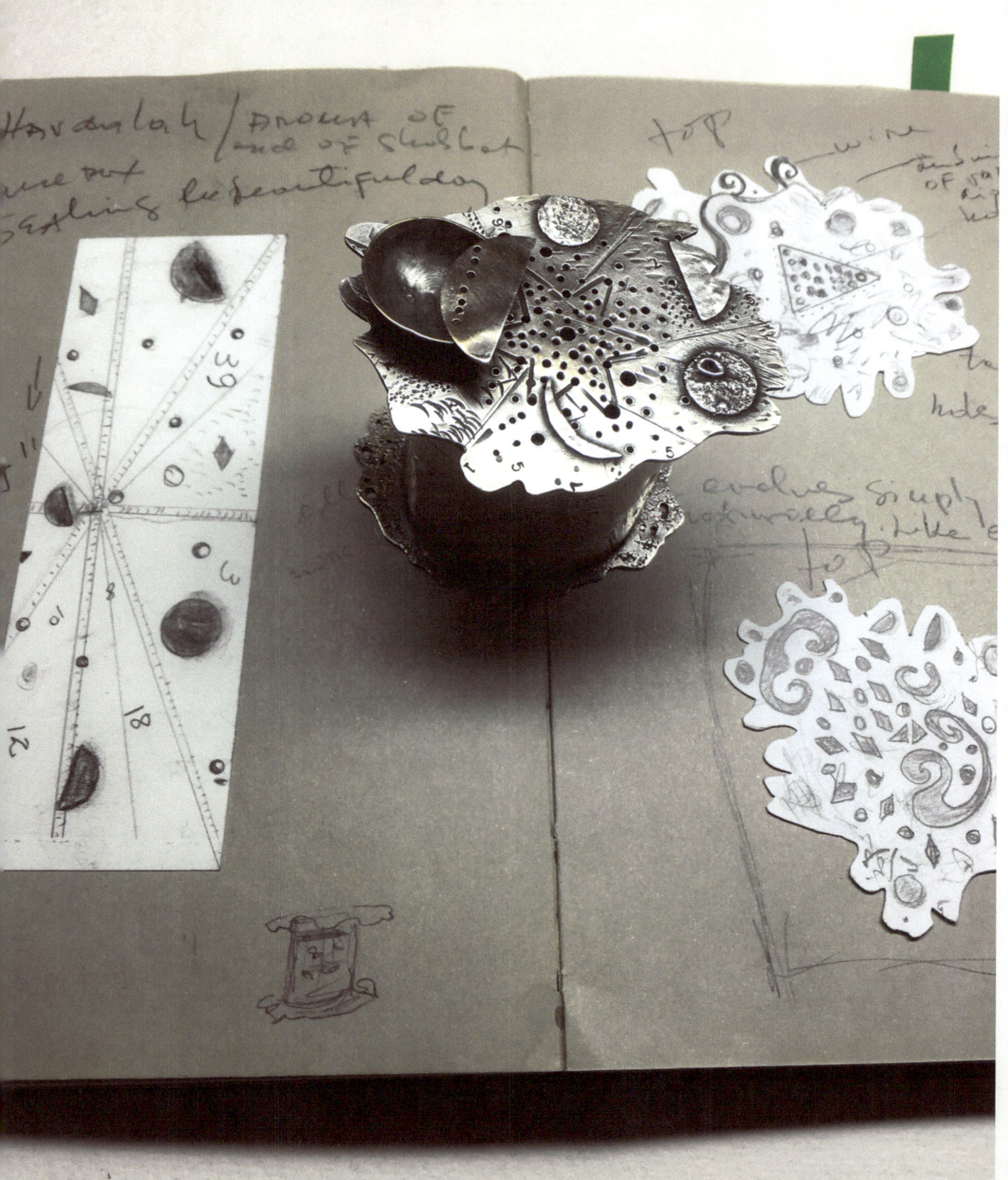

Havdalah Spice silver box with moon cicles.

The sun and the moon give us our shadow at different times of the day.

You can't hide behind your shadow

Shadows are our companion

How can a shadow be the subject of poetry?; painting makes a shadow real because it remains on the surface unchanged

Memories are like painted shadows that remain present.

You Shadow is elusive and dependent on the light behind you — focus, you can control your shadow, where it goes, but not how big it is!

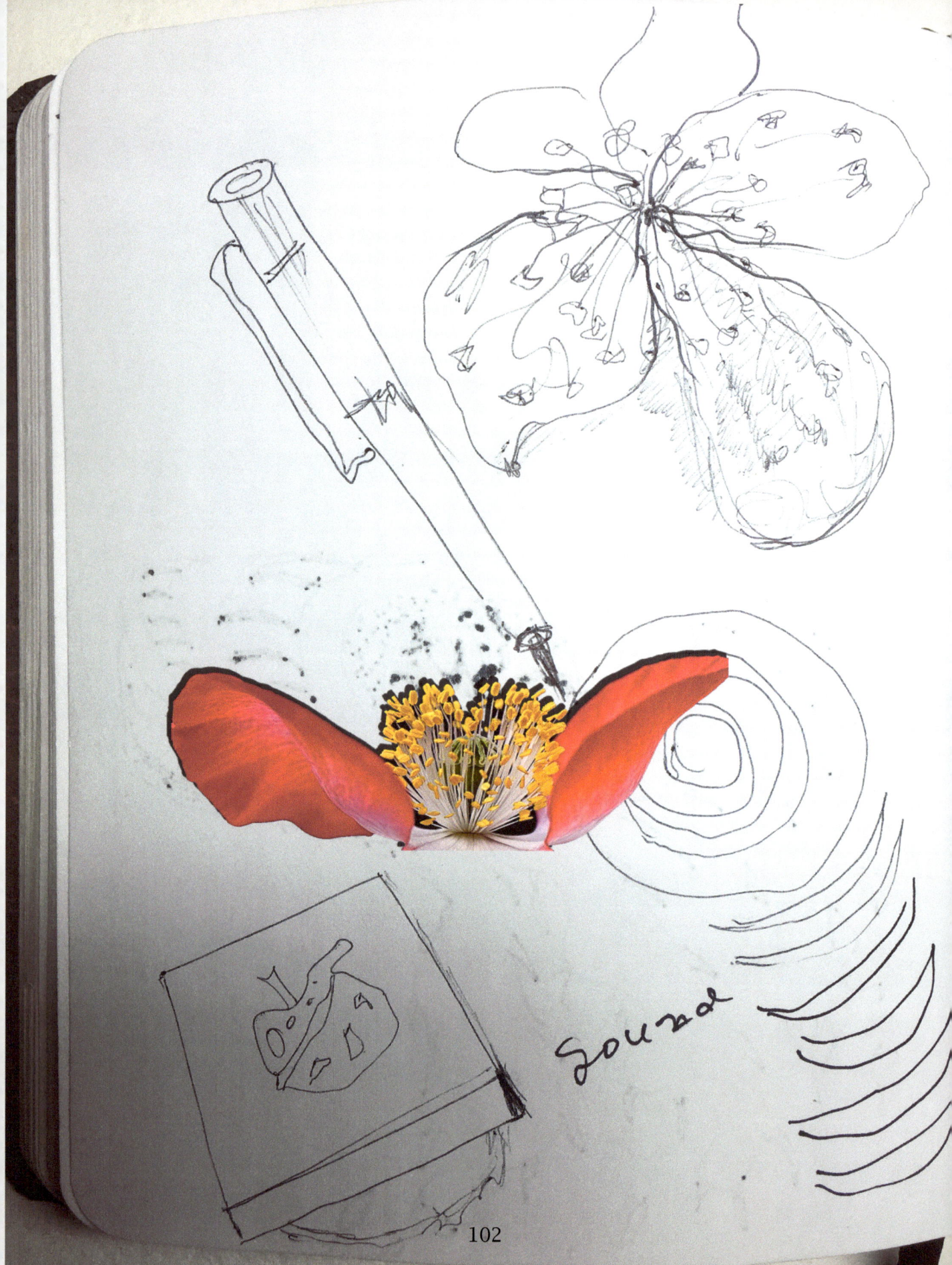

What is the point of form if it's at the expense of function? You cannot sacrifice expression or ornament in what we may call an art piece. Minimalism lacks ornamentation or visual description. The description of a minimalist art piece is more in all the words used to give the significance or the visual context. Should a visual piece just be visual for the viewer and leave the words about it to the critics?

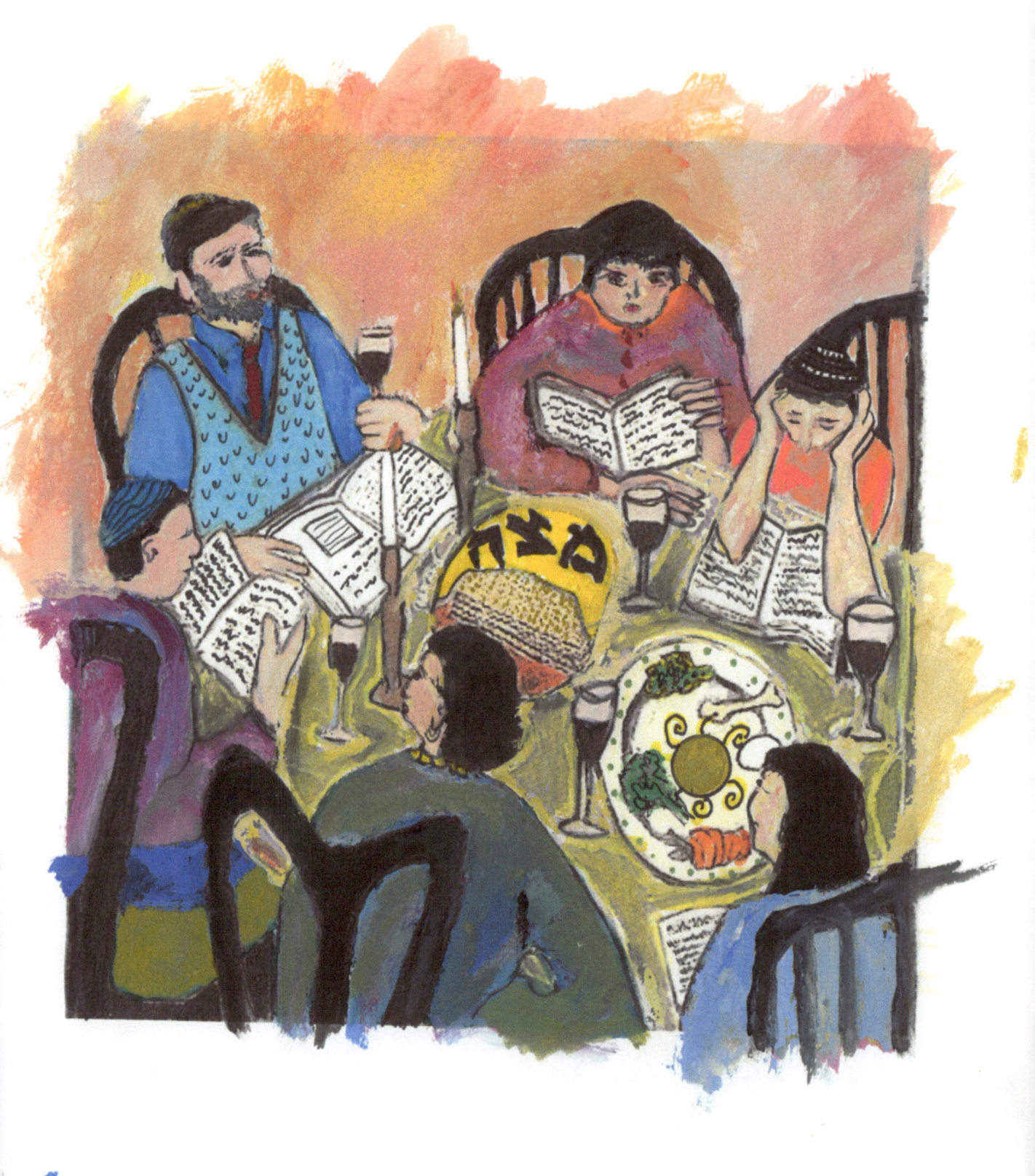

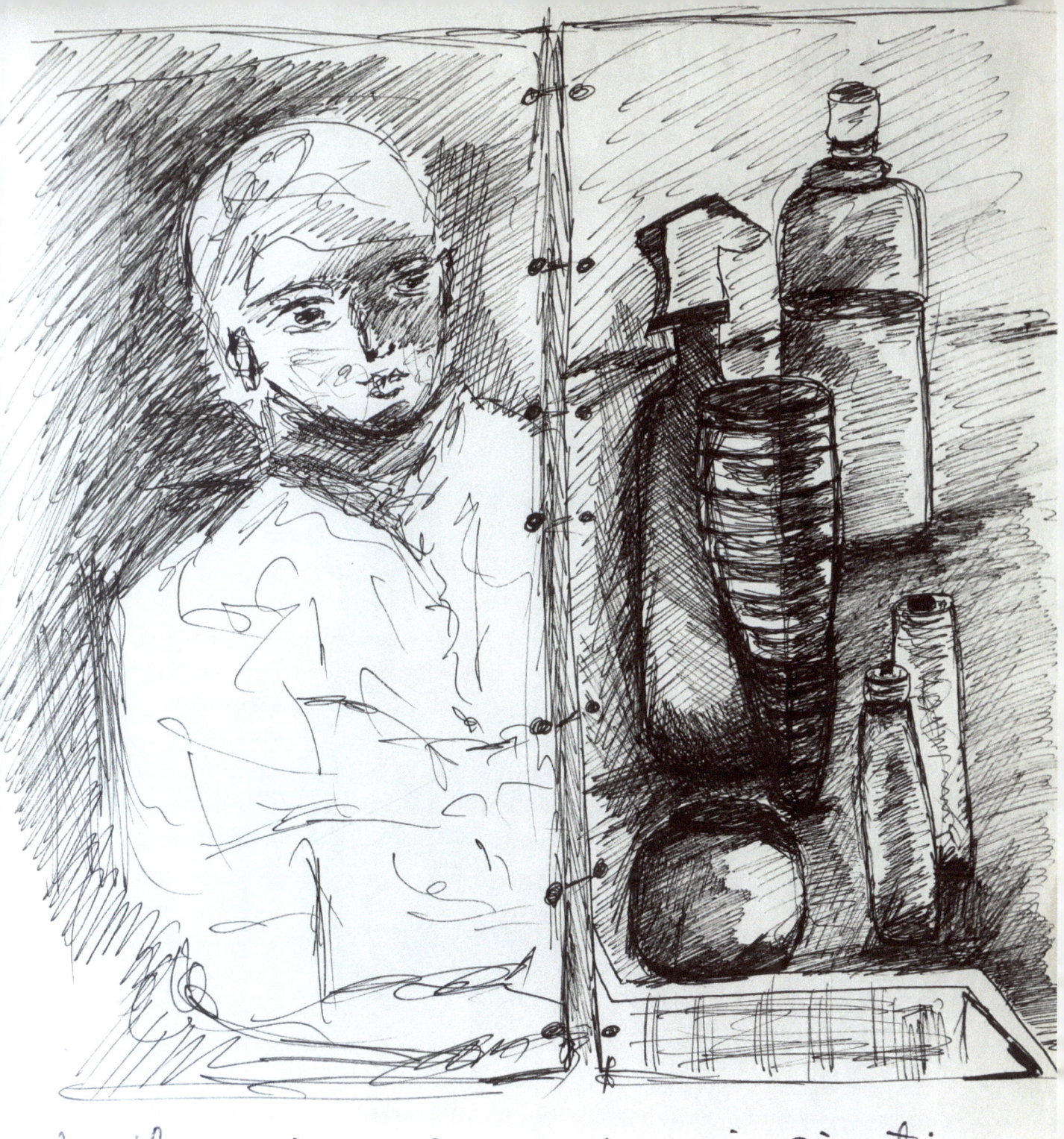

Anything is a source of inspiration
I am reading J. B. Jehoshua "A
journey to the End of the Millenium"
and the images are wonderful. they
allowed for a lot of imagination, Dream..

empty –

dolor
blow –
pain

All my concerts had no sounds in them: they were completely silent. People had to make their own music in their minds.
— Yoko Ono, musician

photo of Dreamer
I embrace the absurd

Bastons

STAFFS
power –

Mirar la ventana del whitney
edificios en DALLAS. Arquitectura
dibujos de arquitectura. blue prints
papel azul con cuadrícula

mental POWER
A ⇄ B
MATERIALISTIC power
ENVIRONMENTAL power

A single event - the EXODUS - key to the whole of Judaism. crucial point in which the Divine errupts into History.

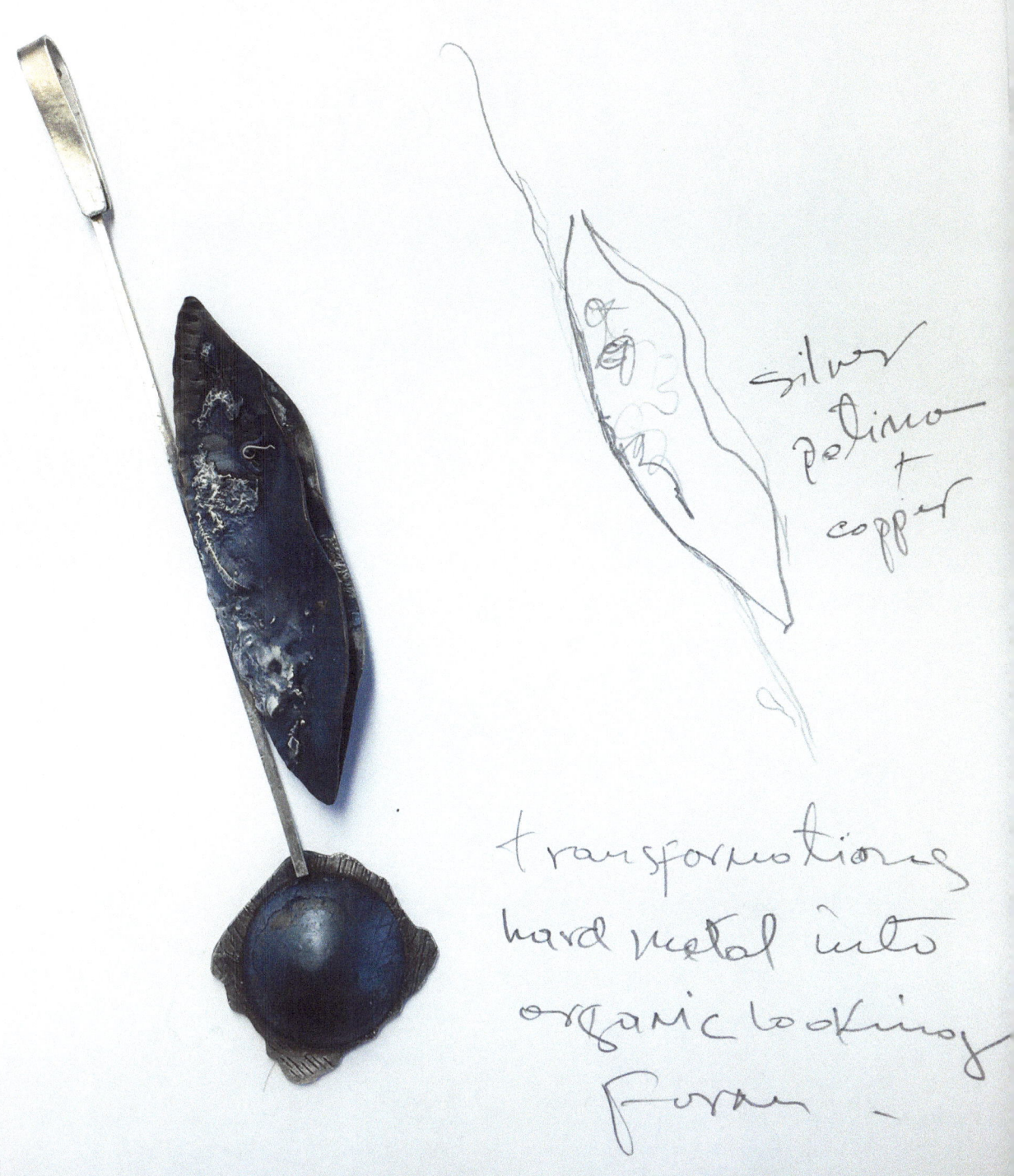

silver patina + copper

transformations hard metal into organic looking form -

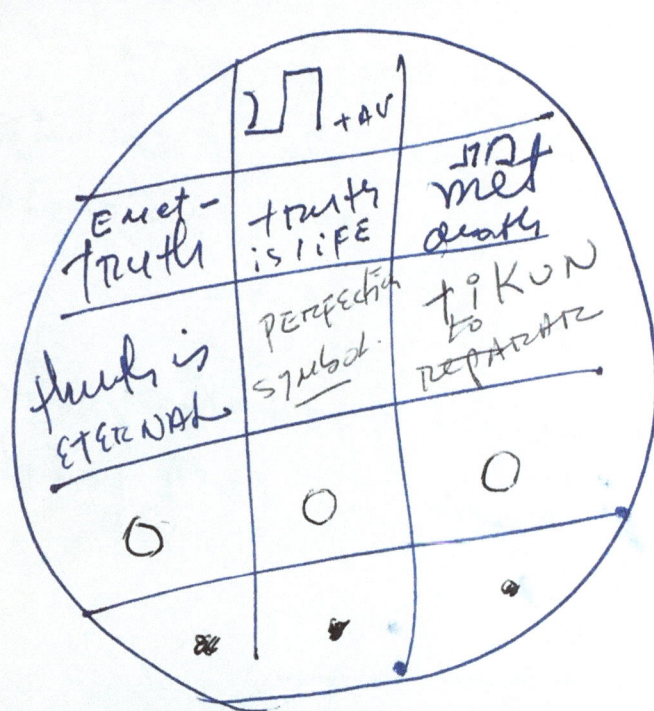

Falshood is not the opposite of truth — it is its Absence —

What is a void...? Darkness? negative space?
How can I play with the void in art?

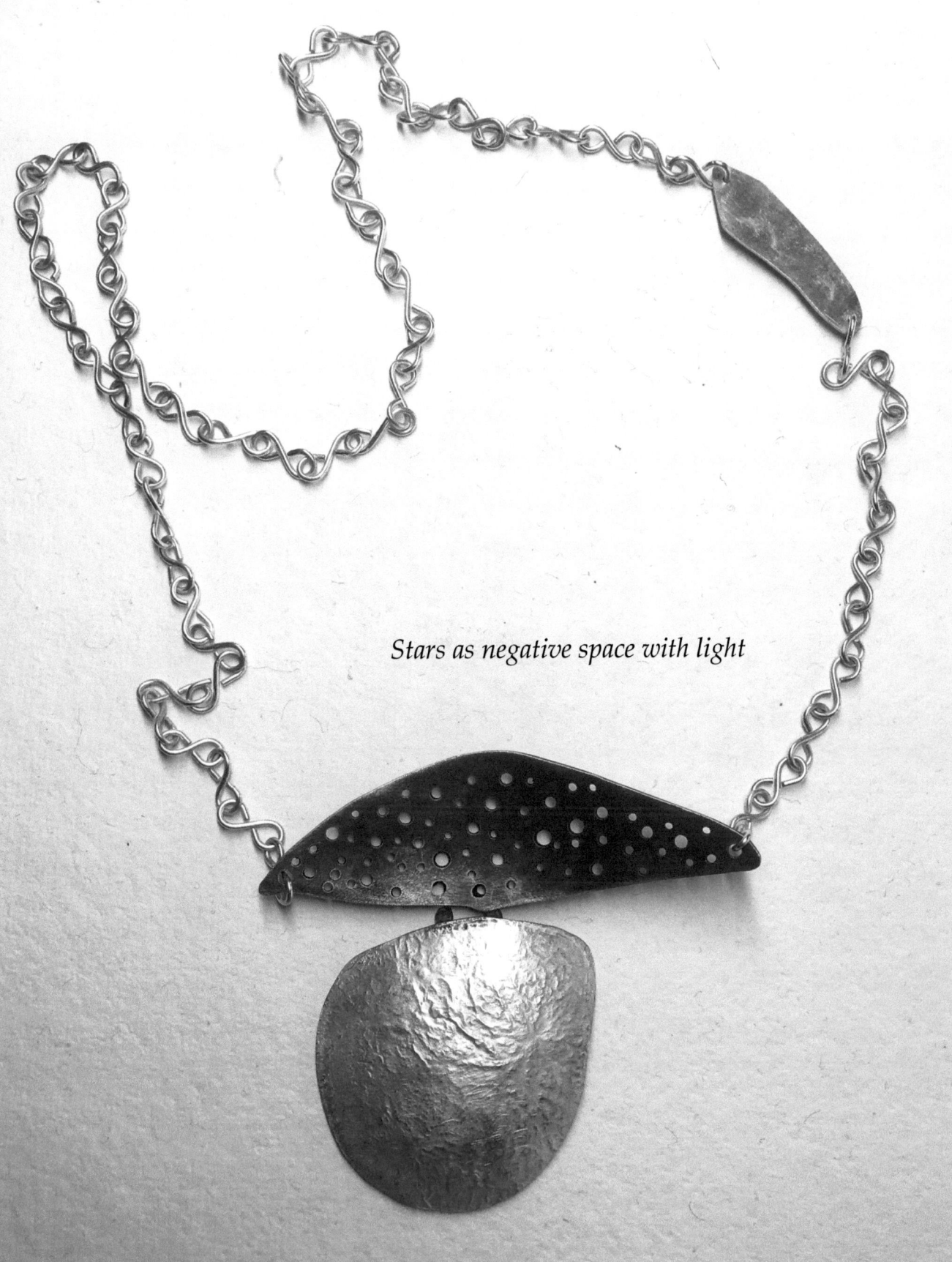

Stars as negative space with light

What is Nostalgia....
beauty and memory...
the "void" with adornment

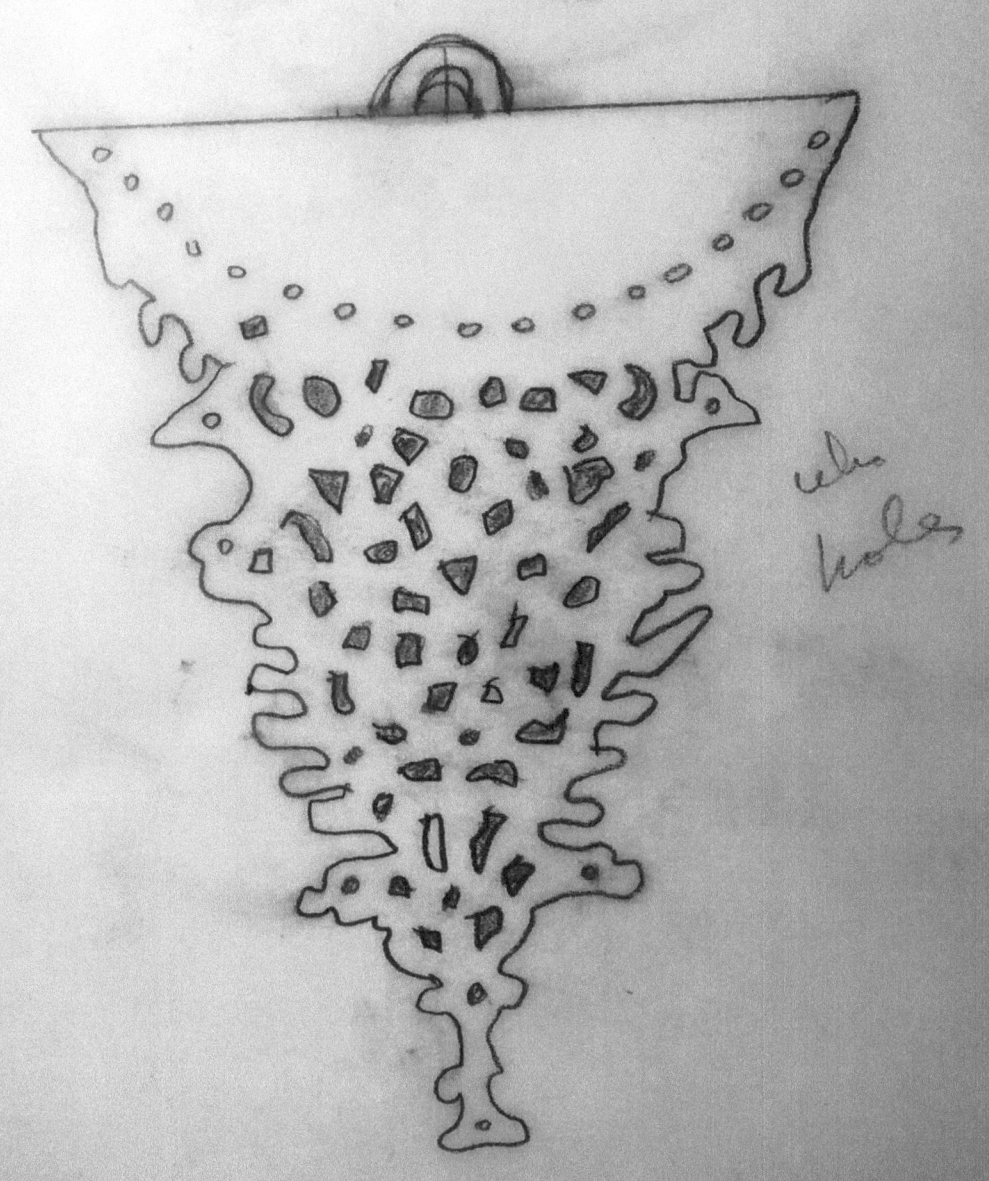

you can create all what you can imagine

longing for vanished worlds
memory / myth —

CAN A PAST that has slipped out of reach be reclaimed by means of Nostalgia?

REflective Nostalgia ①
↓
longing and loss the imperfect process of remembering —
_____

②

Restorative Nostalgia
↓
DANGEROUS — seeks to resuscitate the past as rigorously as possible
↓
Nationalistic revivals

No matter what, the lilies always die!
Life is too short and beauty is fleeting.
We cannot capture the beauty of nature in its full intensity in a moment, only when it's frozen in time.
Is that what photography is?

Proust - remembering things past or rehearsing what's going to happen.

He does not approach the present. It's too difficult to tackle. I know, about the rest? Memory - Proust's destination? Ambiguity.

Proust loves the ambiguity of Monet's painting. He worked like an artist

In his physical writing, he would add, alter, re-memory elements by cutting on a posting on the paper his new thoughts — 1871 D.

Memory and remembering is like falling leaves and the time it takes for them to settle on a surface

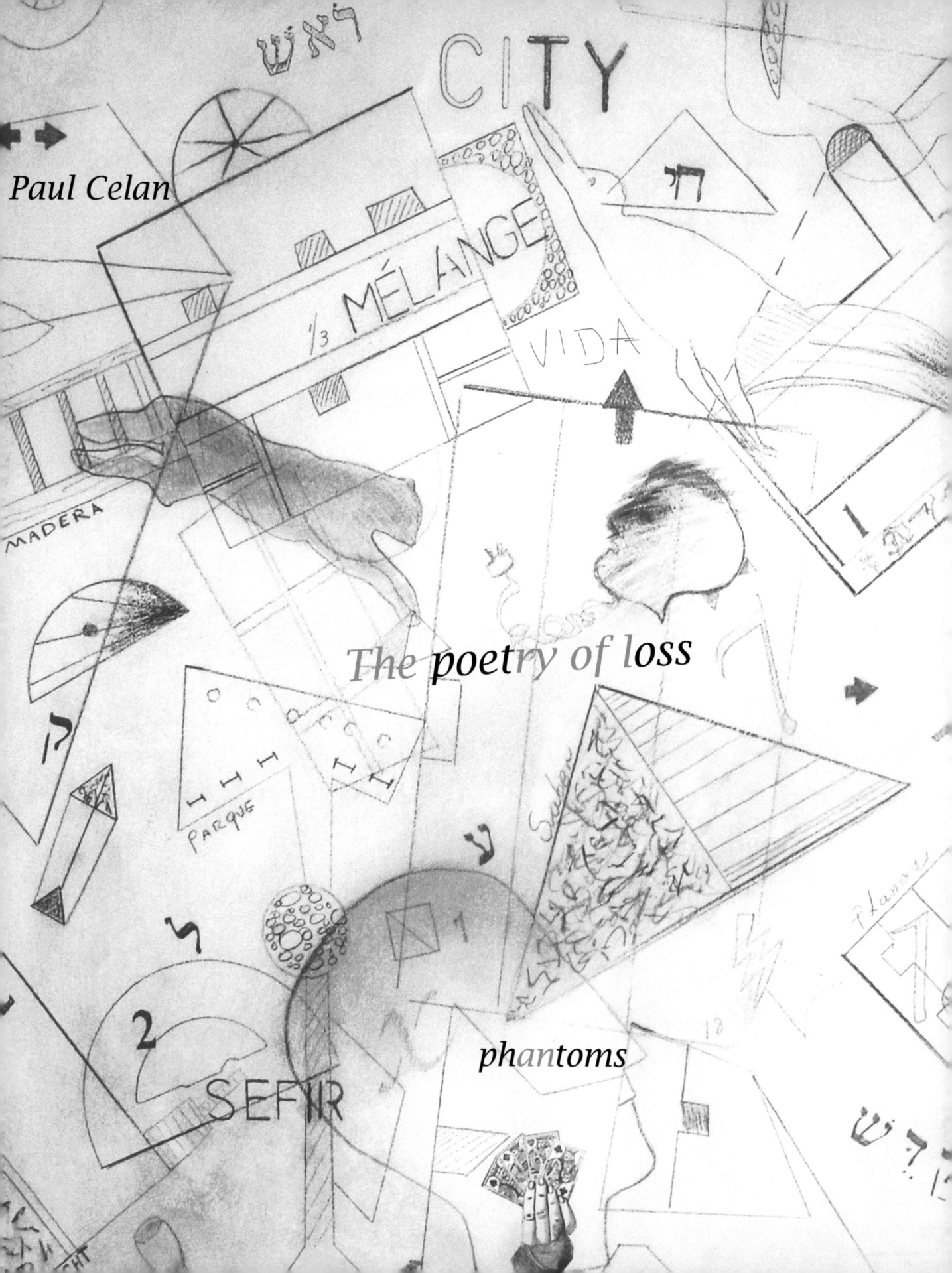

"Black Milk" - Paul Celan's poem

An art piece is a kind of poetry specially if it's quiet!
An object has a memory - a history. Who has the object has a story and a history. That is why we get so attached to our objects. They remind us of our history.
The uprooted and the disappeared are the phantoms that inhabit us. And silence is the way of communication of our phantoms....
Dreaming memories.

genius of words

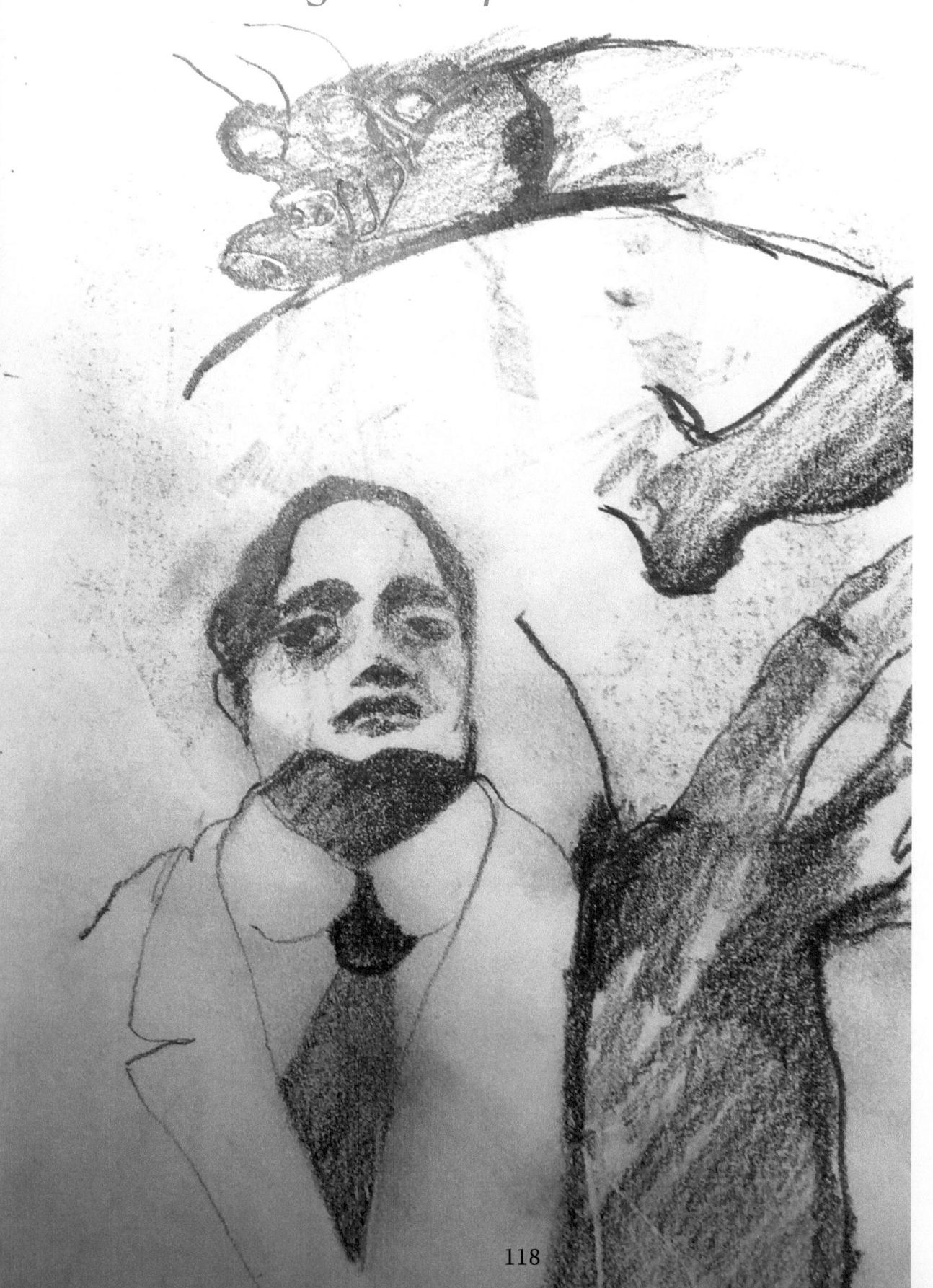

Garcia Lorca

reinvigorated poetry
the torrentially expresive
poet. left us beauty and
genius of words.

(Ghosts + Acrobatics) we do acrobatics all the time —

concern è human existence, within a physical emotional + psychological environment,

man's constant hope in a search for liberation from the anxiety of our times.

Dos moniques sin cabeza minapez.

If you dream of clouds...

Alienation produces eccentrics... or... Revolutionaries in whatever field —

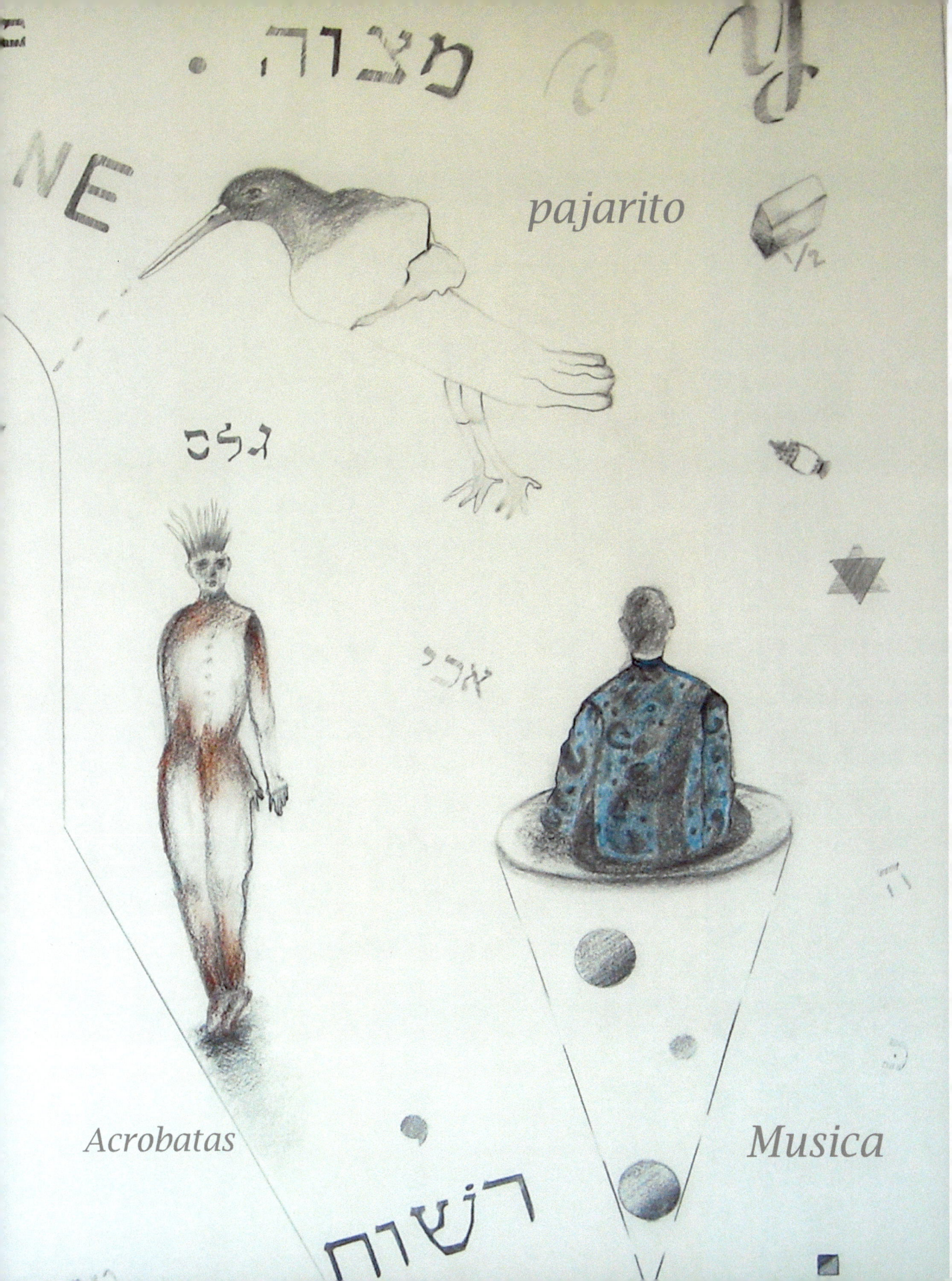

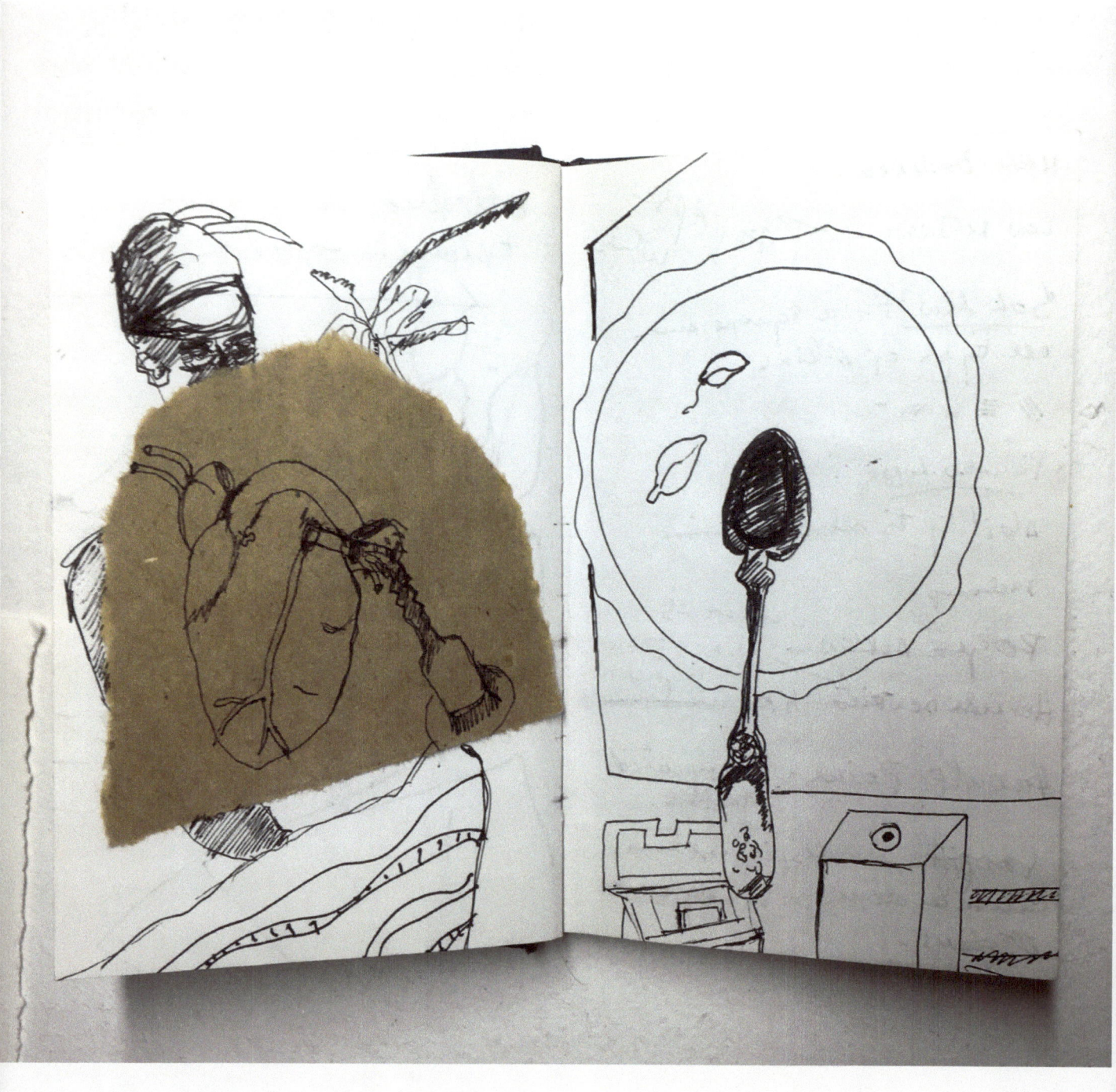

Contrast and ambiguity are part of my aesthetic pursuit. Ambiguity gives a chance to create different narratives, which is feasible when drawing from the life experiences of each viewer.

Morocco for me is a pinacle of ambiguity. My heart pounds with excitement with the cognitive dissonances I experience day in and day out.

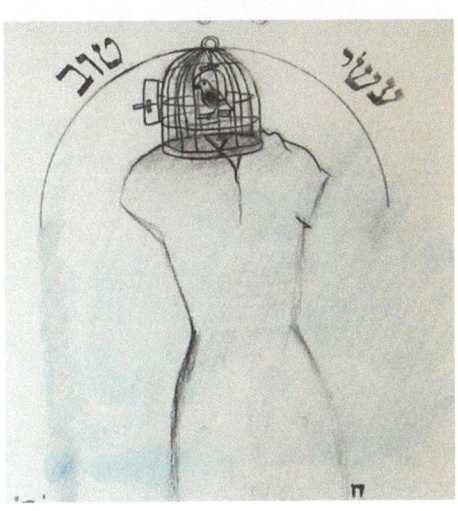

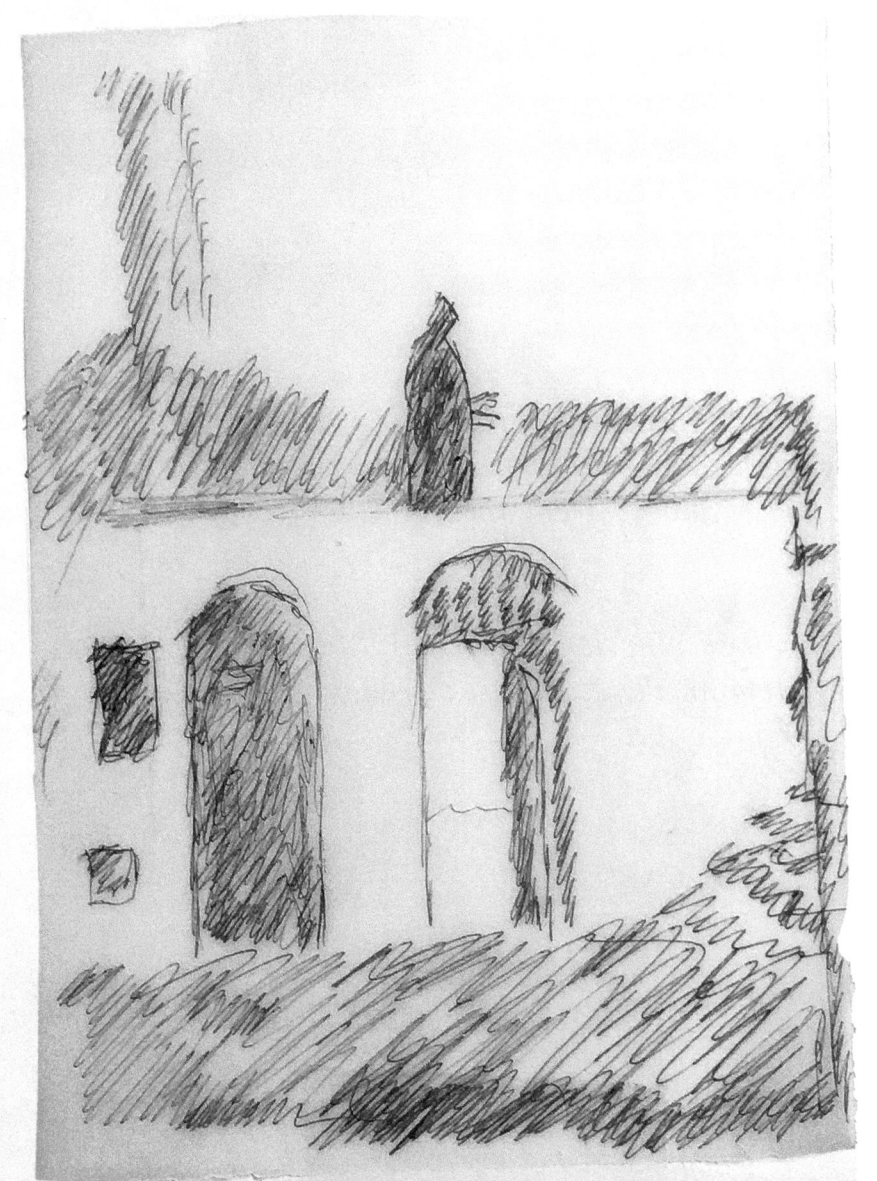

Solitude of mind and body (?) to be in the world with the sea in front to reflect and think and create in your own time. How important to be with yourself and your thoughts! ♡

Jewish Mysticism

Reflection + interpretation of a text

calibrated bezel
c zirconium

meats at market in
FEZ, Morocco

Reacting to Religion Norman
Mailer — wrote about Hassidic
stories of Martin Buber.
MALAMUD — American successor
of Bashevis Singer Yiddish Stories
of sin — guilt — redemption...

BOETHIUS —

An imaginary wing to fly -
I think curiosity is the push
to invention

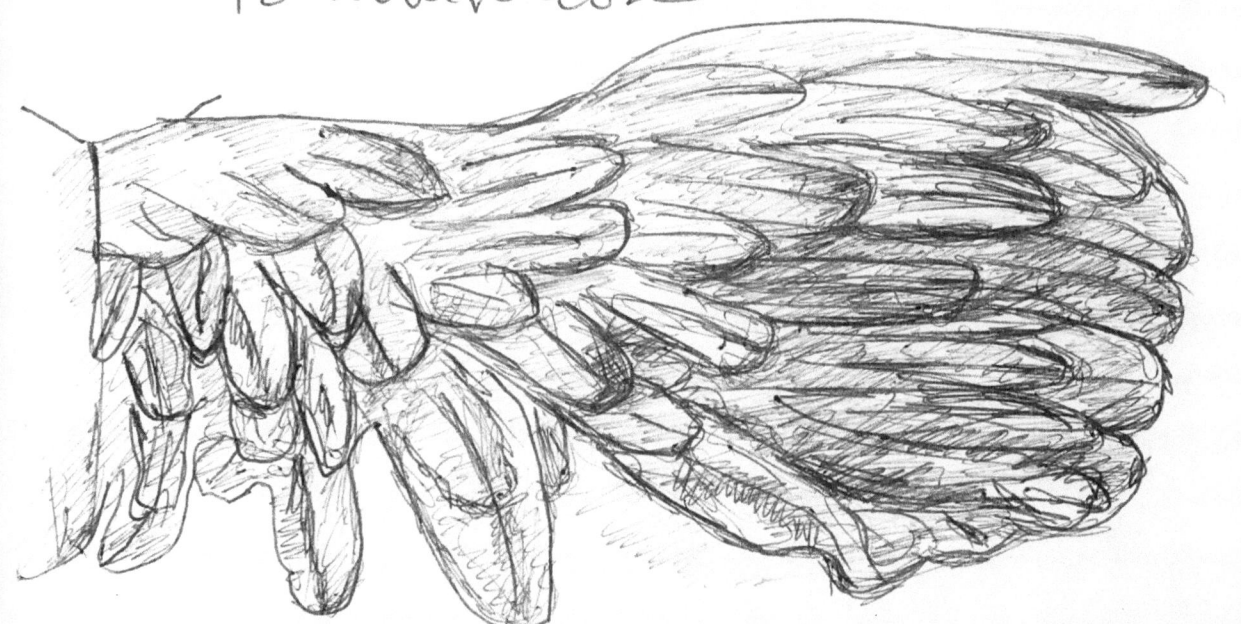

How things work, how does the mind work, what's it that makes every mind work in a different way, How does chemistry and biology "control"(?) what the mind does? How does the mind see things. Why do we see things when we dream, I dreamed of the H brow Alphabet and made a book!

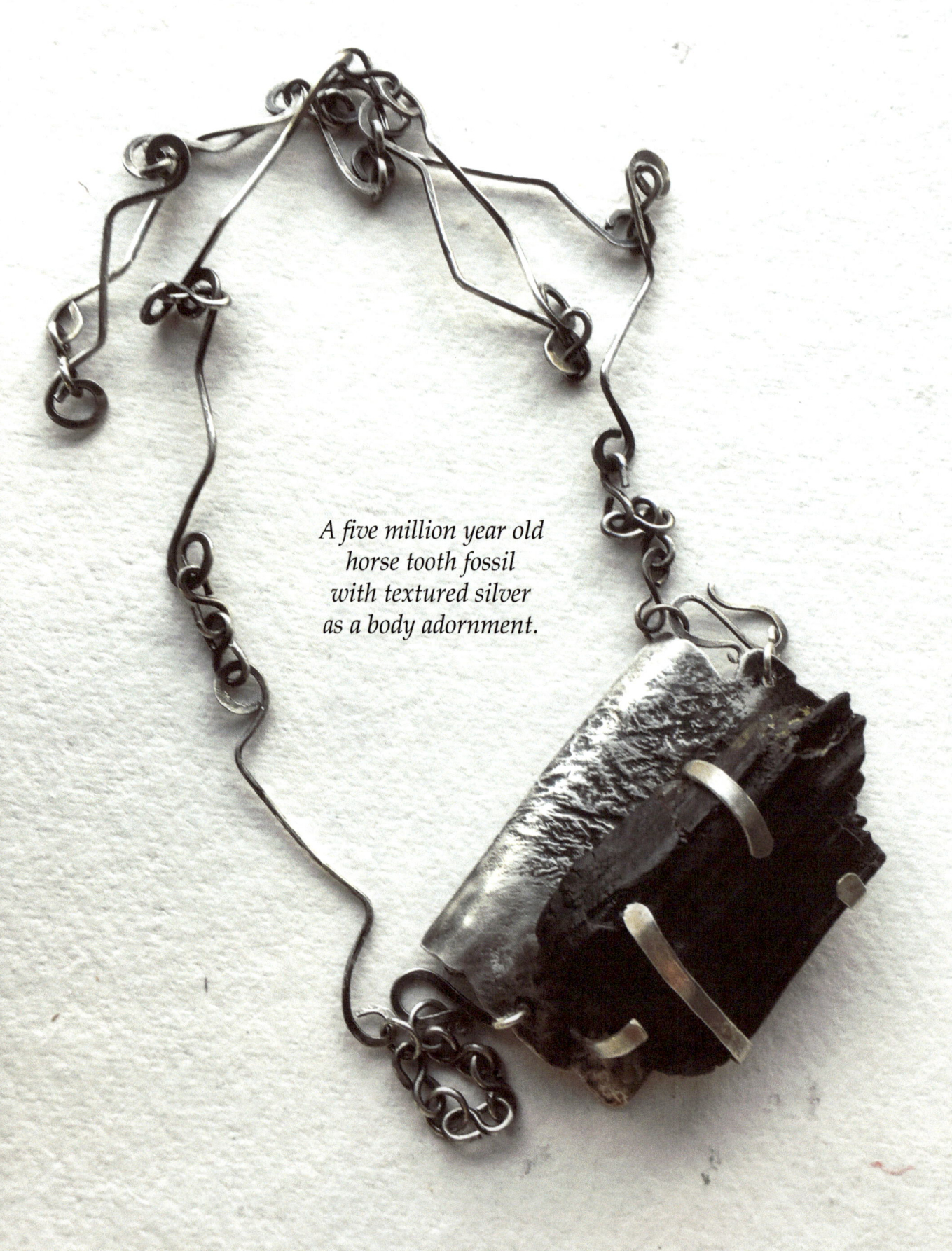

A five million year old horse tooth fossil with textured silver as a body adornment.

Reflective Nostalgia

Layers

Silver

Tape Brooch

white
silver

mirrored

reticulated

BLACK
texture
texture

concave
convex

edge
irregular Brooch

shaped on
wood —
the void is
always present!

organic
shape

fragments make life

Museu Picasso

azul

mesa de pies – 80 120
o pesah — pata de arriba
más obstruida.

Arte civil – Gótico siglo
13 al 15
bordes
cabeza páginas de
libros. placas de
madera
arte gótico.

placas anchas de madera
miran arte gótico con rayos
coros – arte civil.

Hacen pedazos de cemento
con algo si no pesa
relieves.

Ladrillos con vidrio
adentro y negros y ricnet

cuadrado

Pajarito

shaped
pearls —
Ajor silver

STUDIO
wed. 1 - 6.
2:30 - 7:30

אבות

hoja de afseits
tamaños

○ pierce
▲ pierce
△ sweat solder

texture
negative

texture
Negative
texture
texture
Negative

sweat solder
texture
pierce

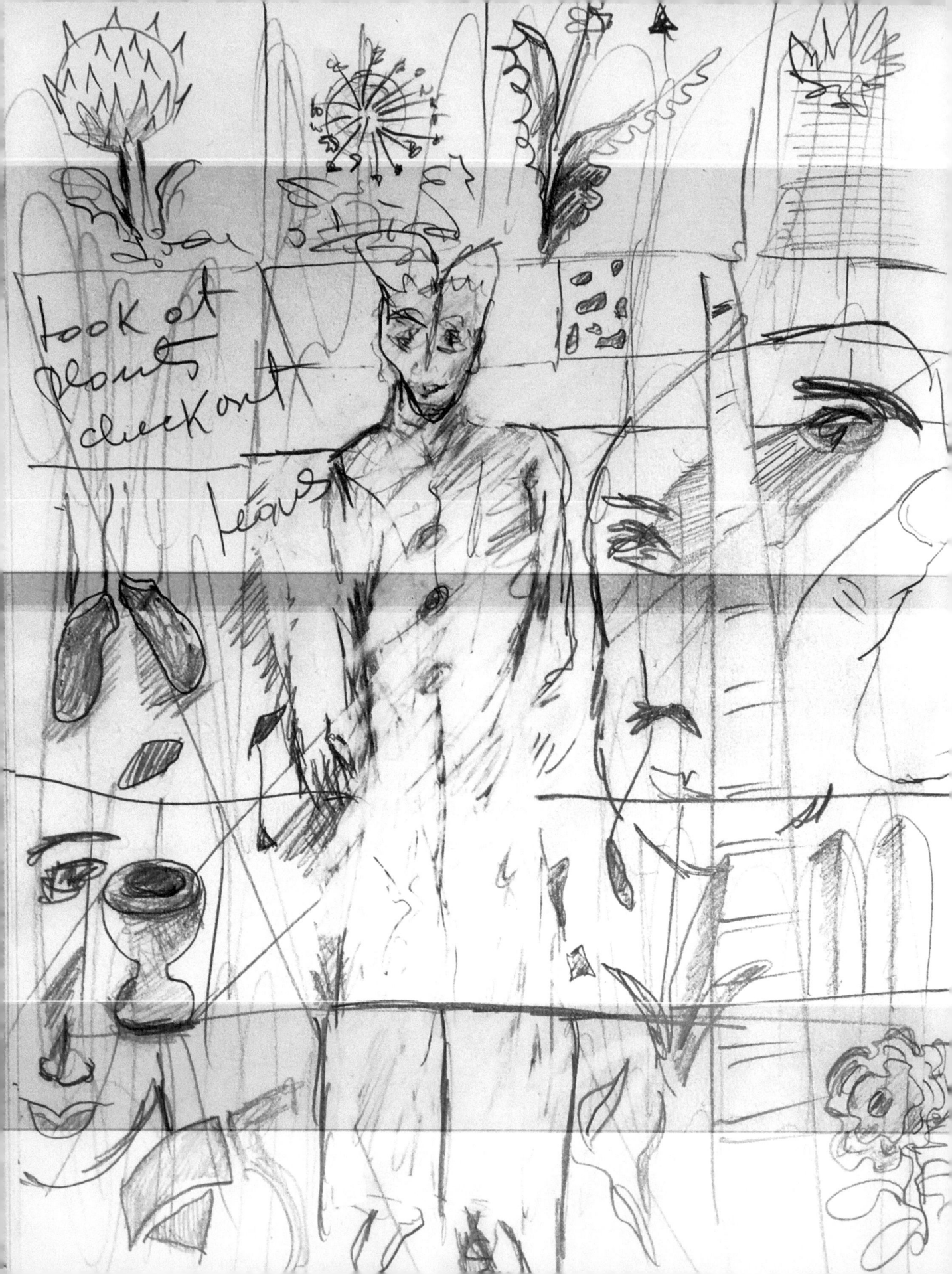

tratar de penetrar
beneath the surface
of things, untuit
human mystery, and
find ways of
embodying the invisible,
inscrutable aspects.

> Sometimes I see it
> and then paint it.
> Other times
> I paint it and
> then see it.
> Both are impure
> situations, and
> I prefer neither.
>
> —Jasper Johns,
> *painter*

La iconog...
para a...
cultura...
una for...
todos r...
símbolos...
miento, l...

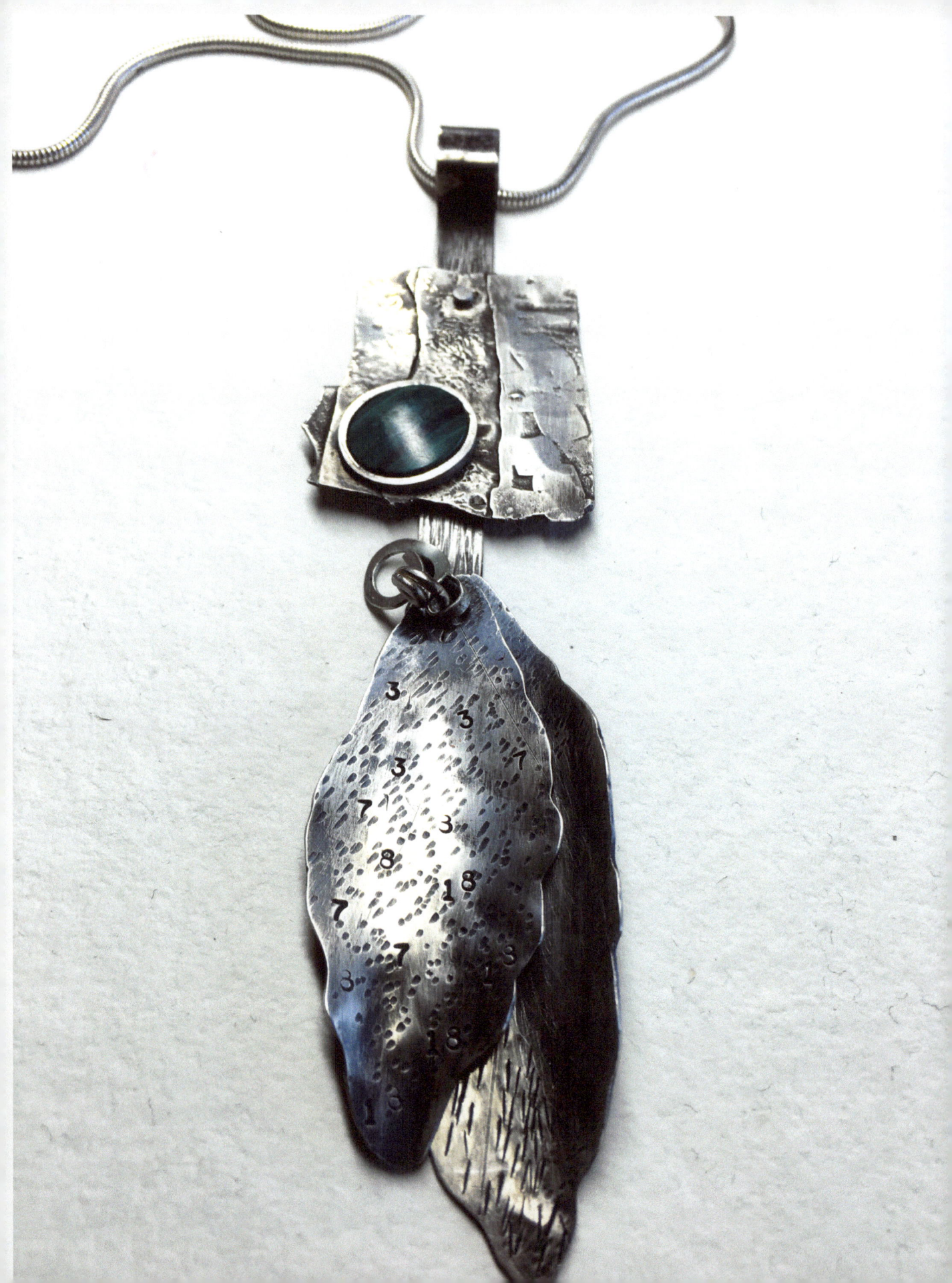

What is creativity —
Art and Science intersect to produce creative effect — objects, ideas

curiosity —
questioning —

How the mind leaps around,

1503 —
environment and diversity is a great phenomenon for creativity

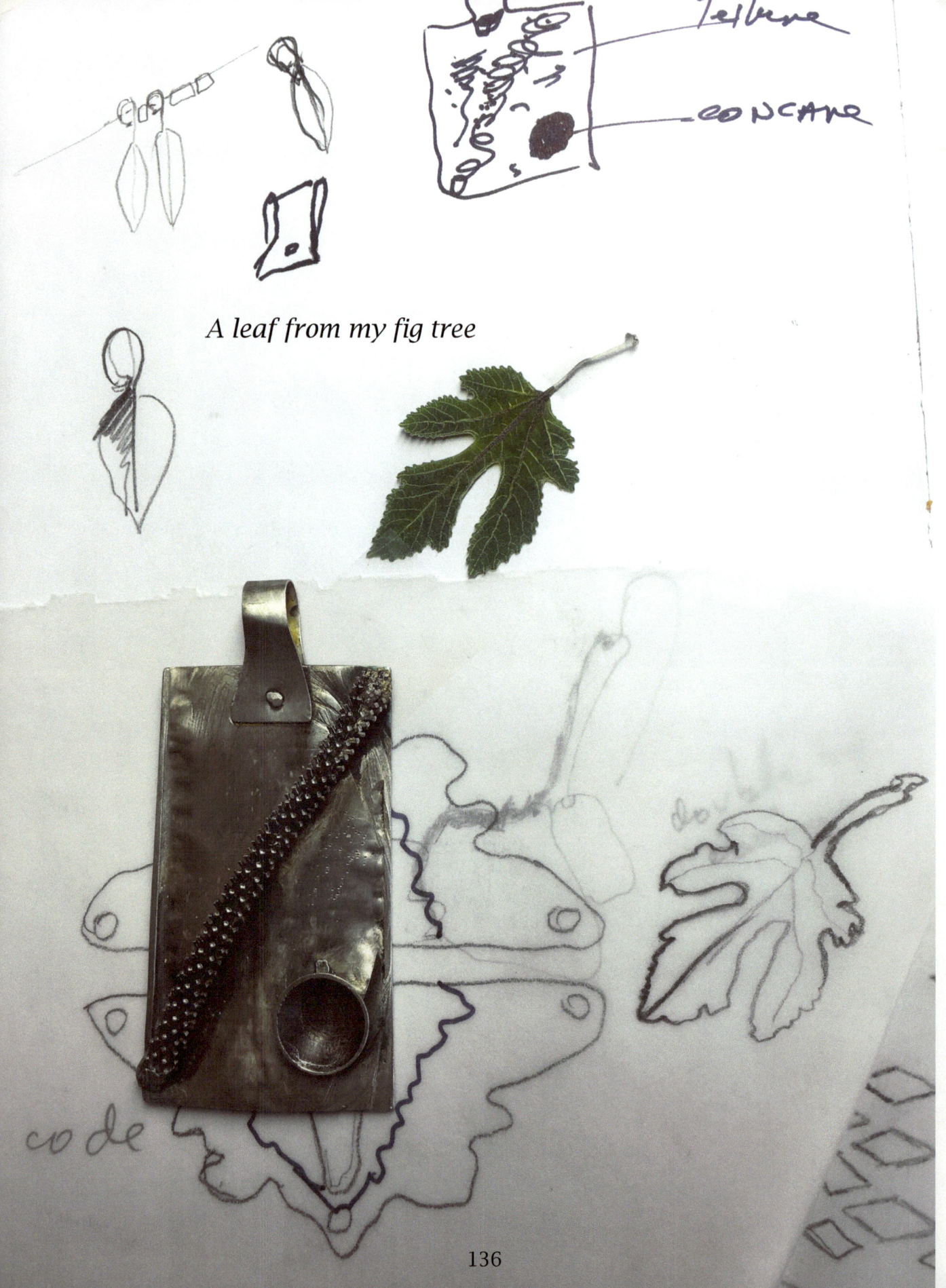

A leaf from my fig tree

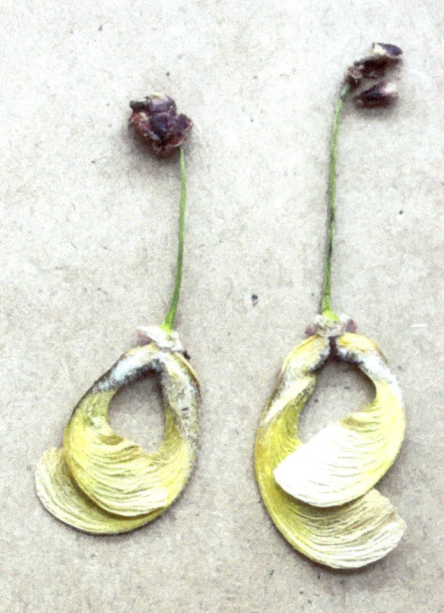

How beautiful!
I picked up these on my walk and left them inside my notebook to dry.
age in nature gives you subtleties and a special beauty.
I so delight in this.
Inspiration for a body silver adornment —

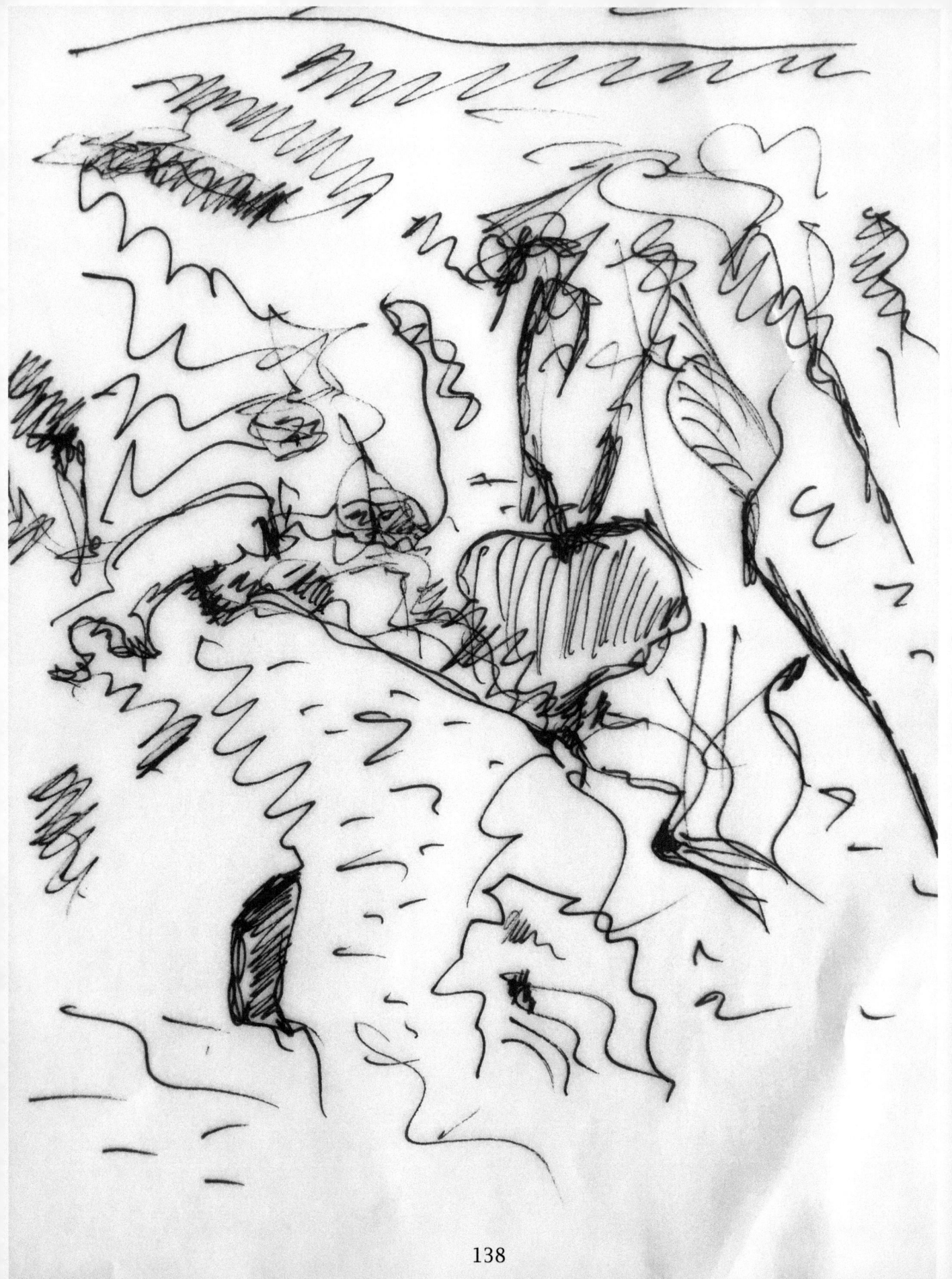

Body adornments sterling silver

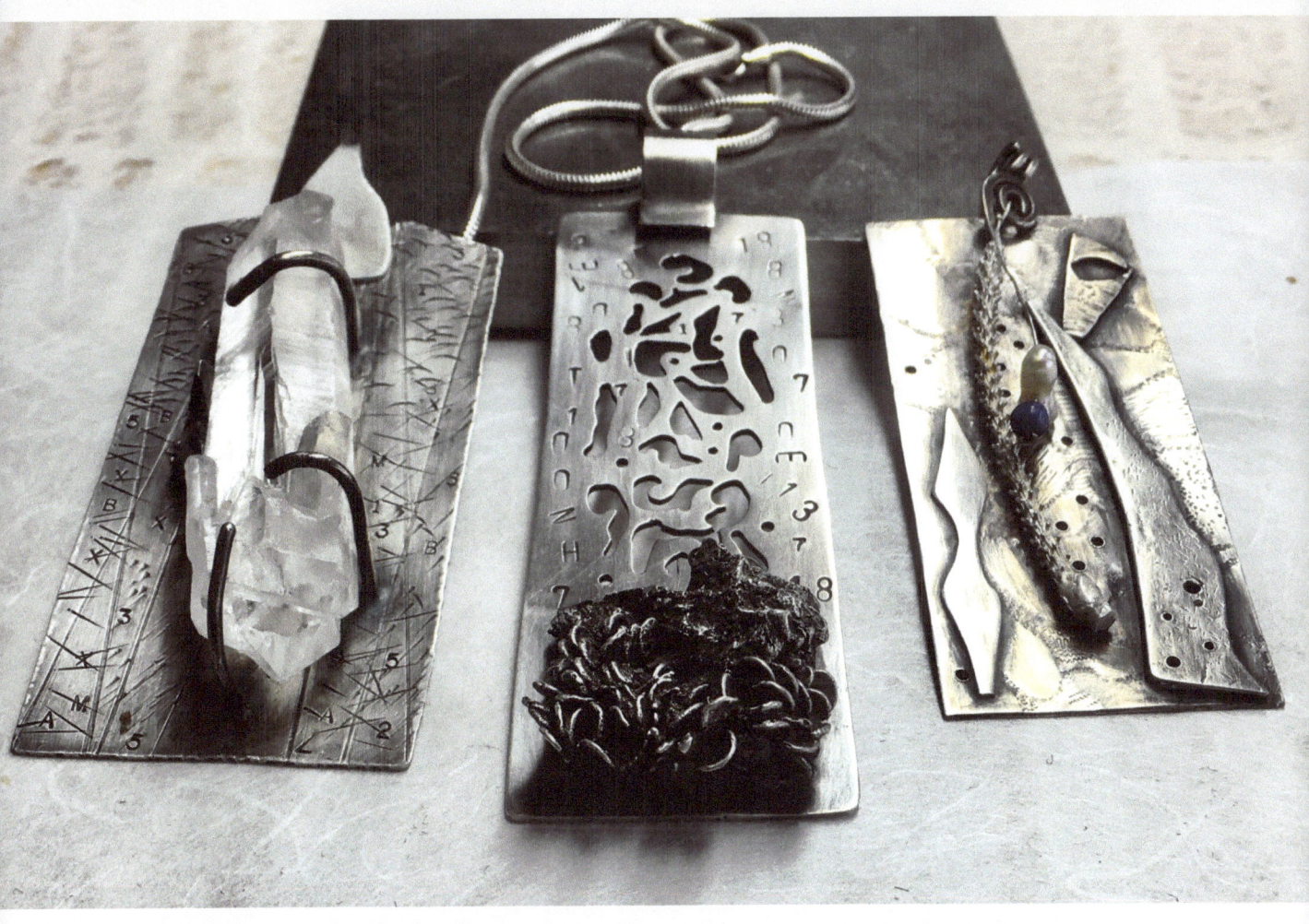

*Landscape
fragmentation
void
texture
numbers
letters
rock crystal
seeds
pearls
lapiz lazuli
patina*

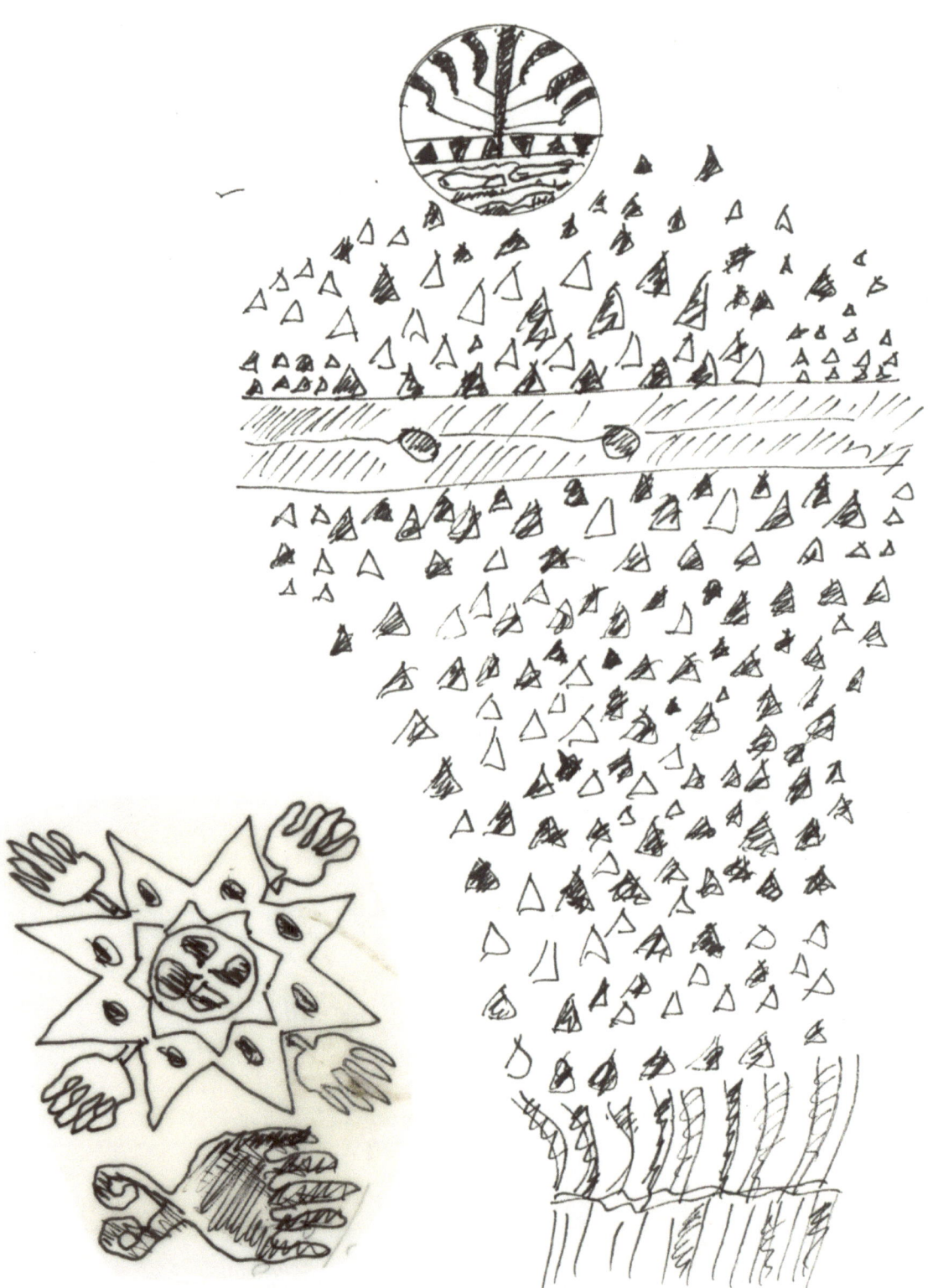

When the actor is at a peak, the audience is in perfect harmony. All their attention is focused on one spot, like in a meditative experience, and I'm sure they're all breathing together.

—Ellen Burstyn, *actress*

I look at the clouds that form in the beautiful sky of Santa Fe, NM. once get inspired by their shapes I was thinking it would be nice to feel embraced by them.

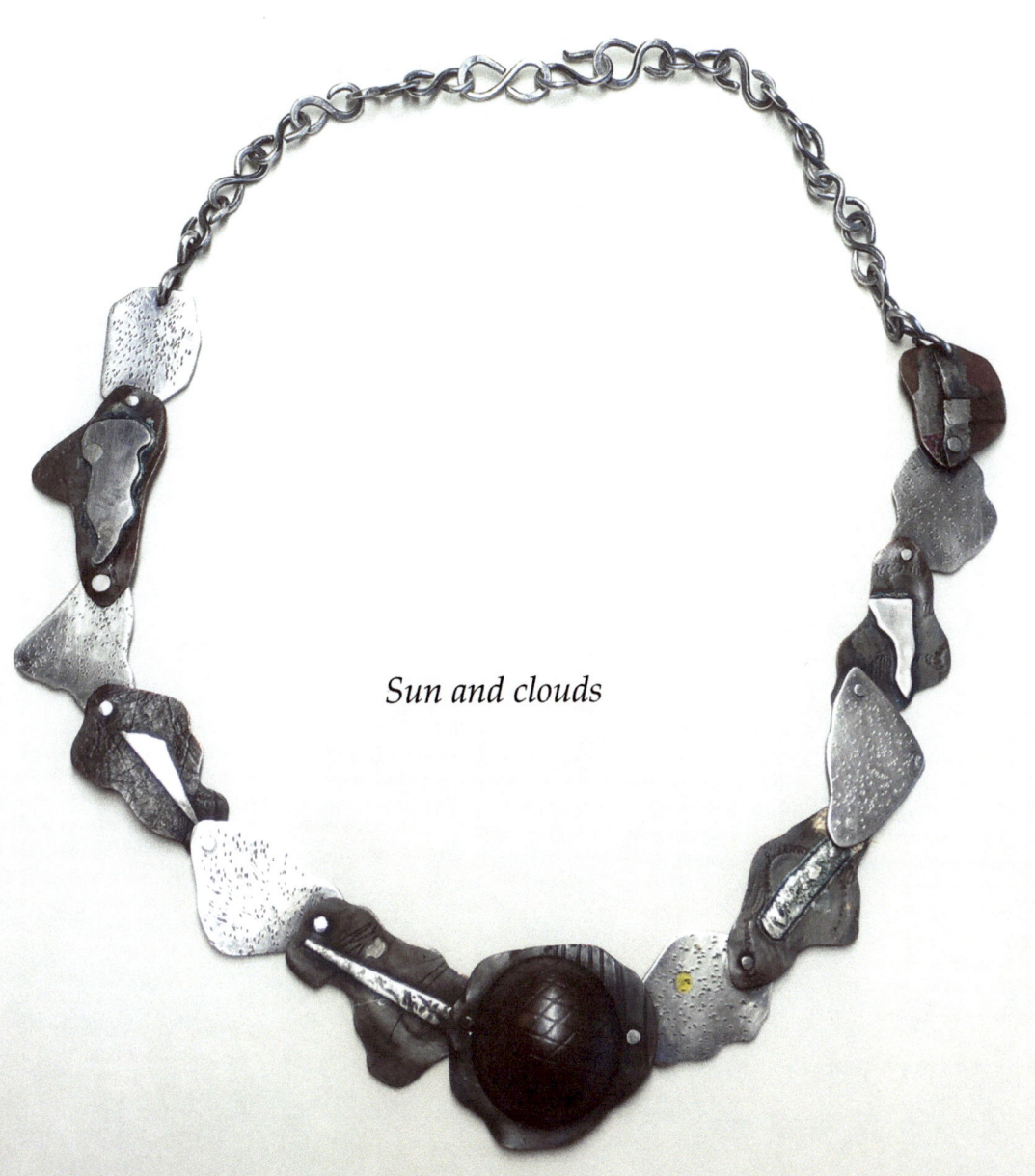

Sun and clouds

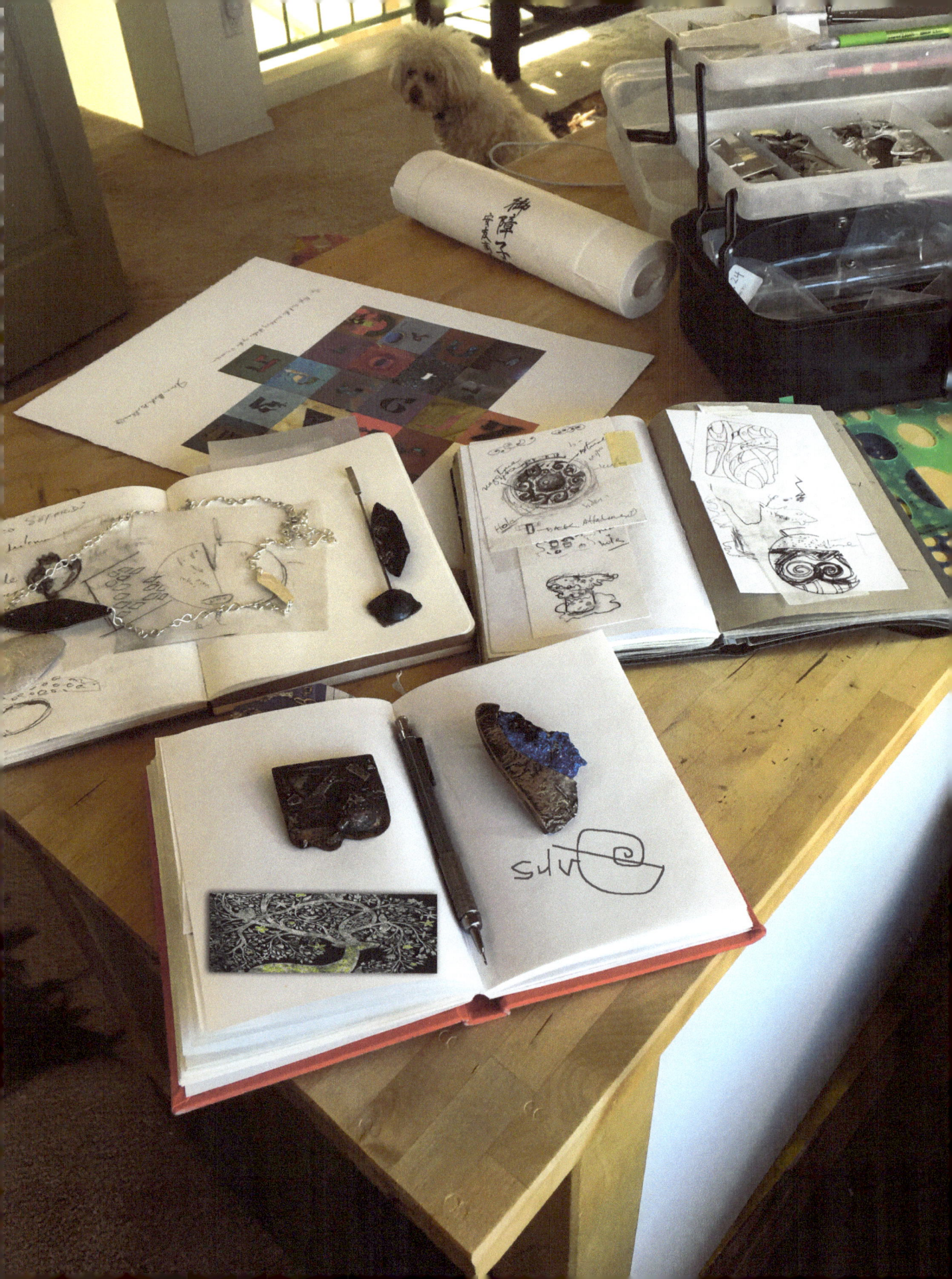

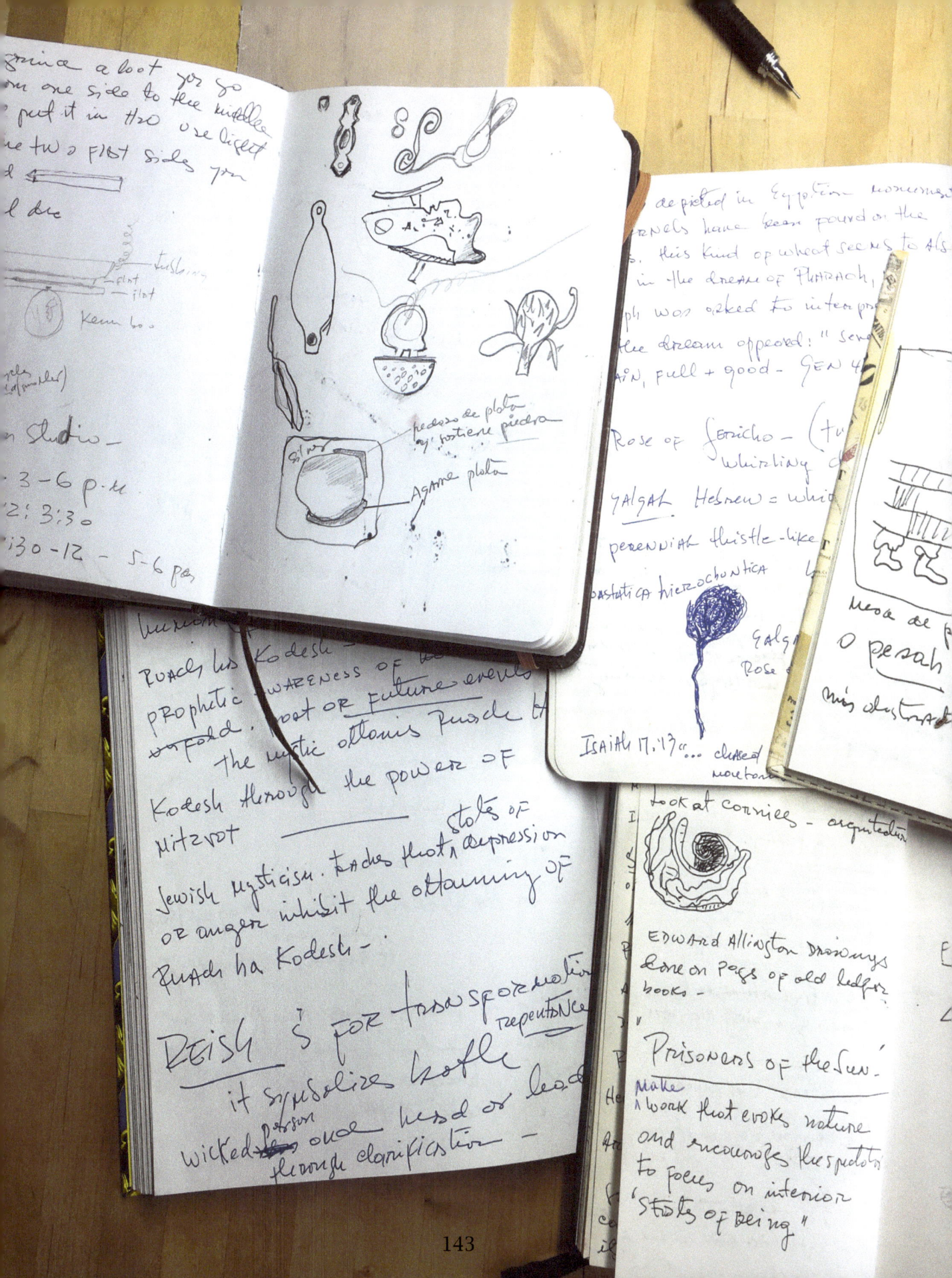

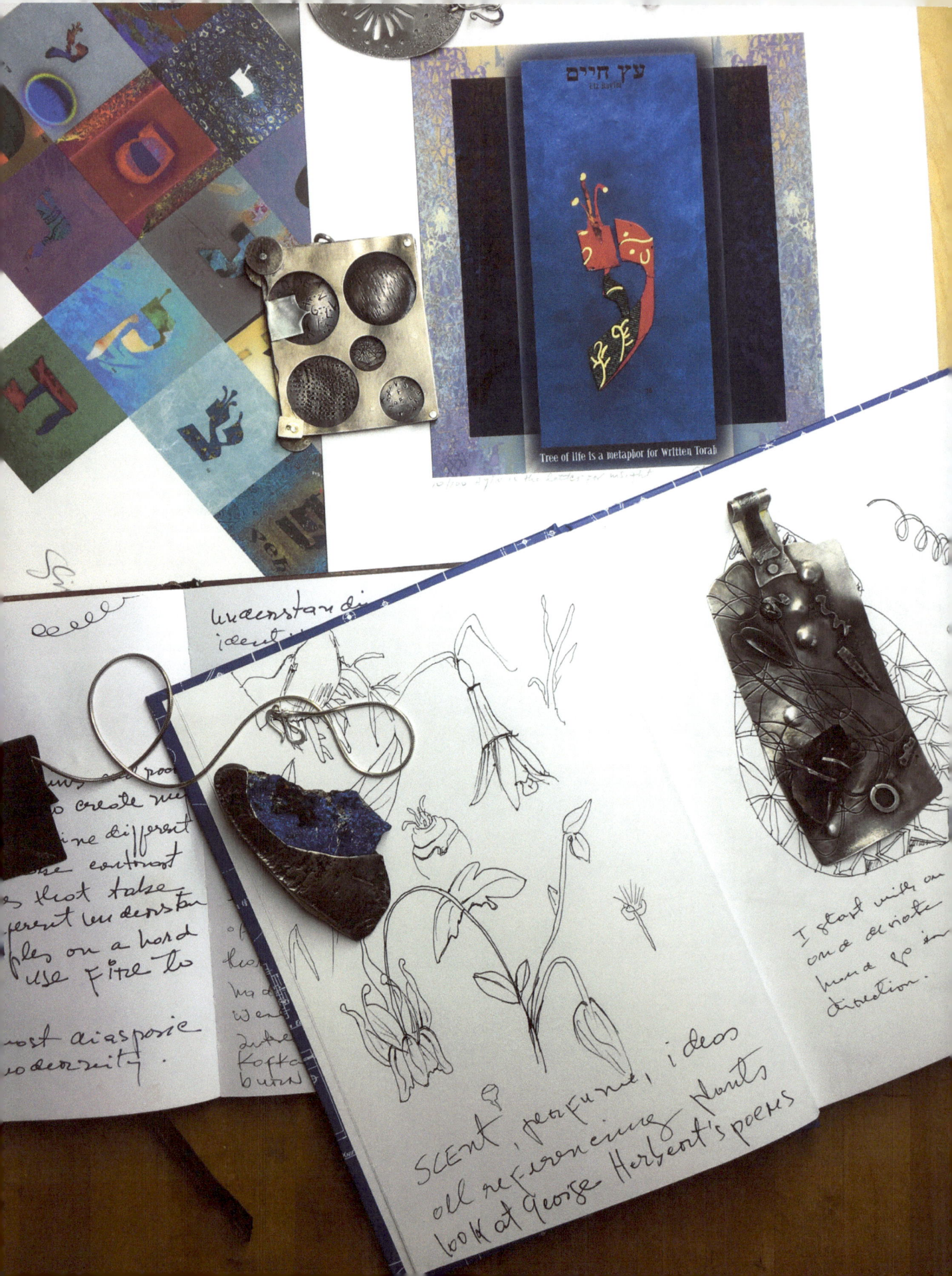

Color is a profoundly beautiful part of the sensuous world.

Color gives us atmospheric feelings of happiness or quietness. Color alters mood.

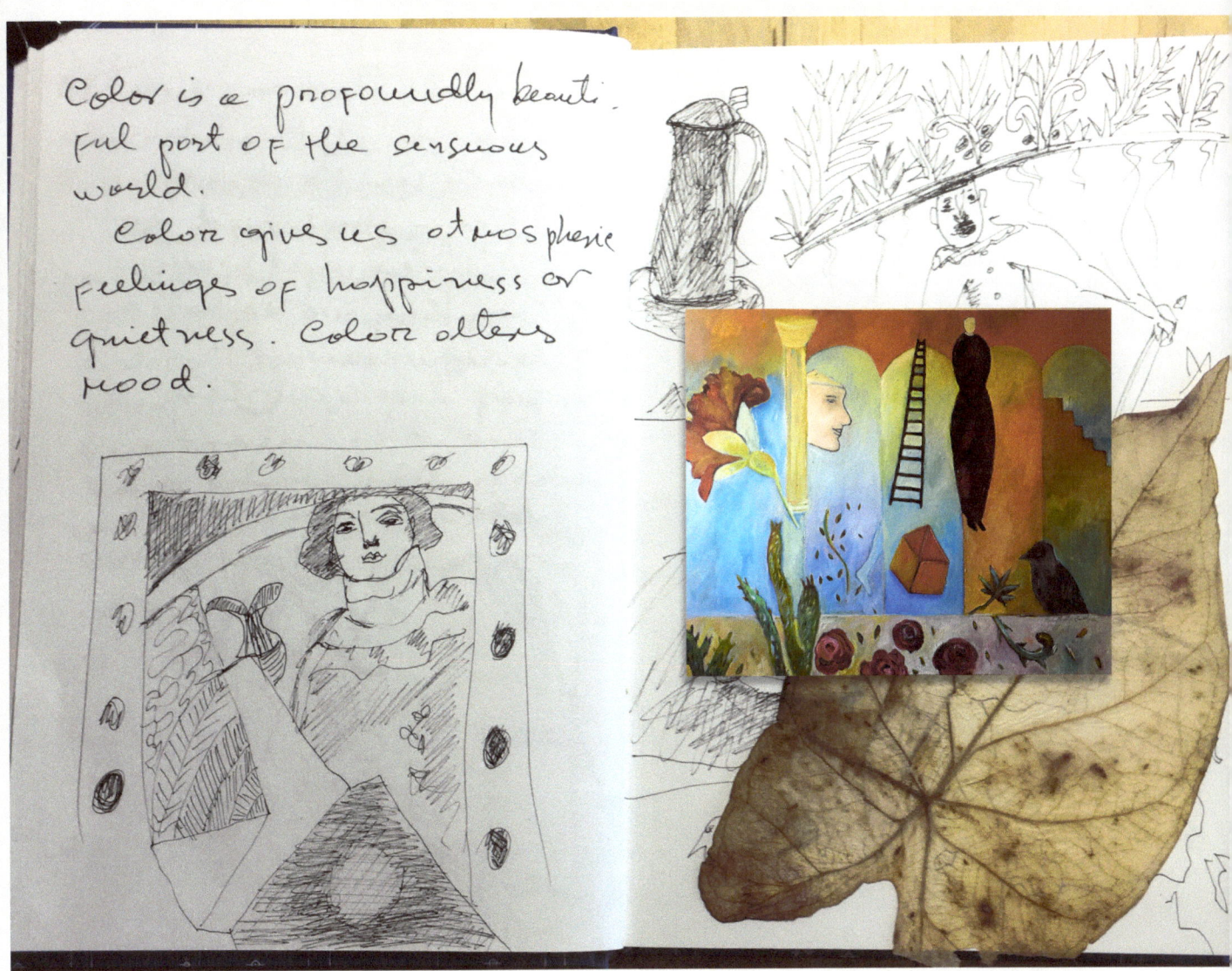

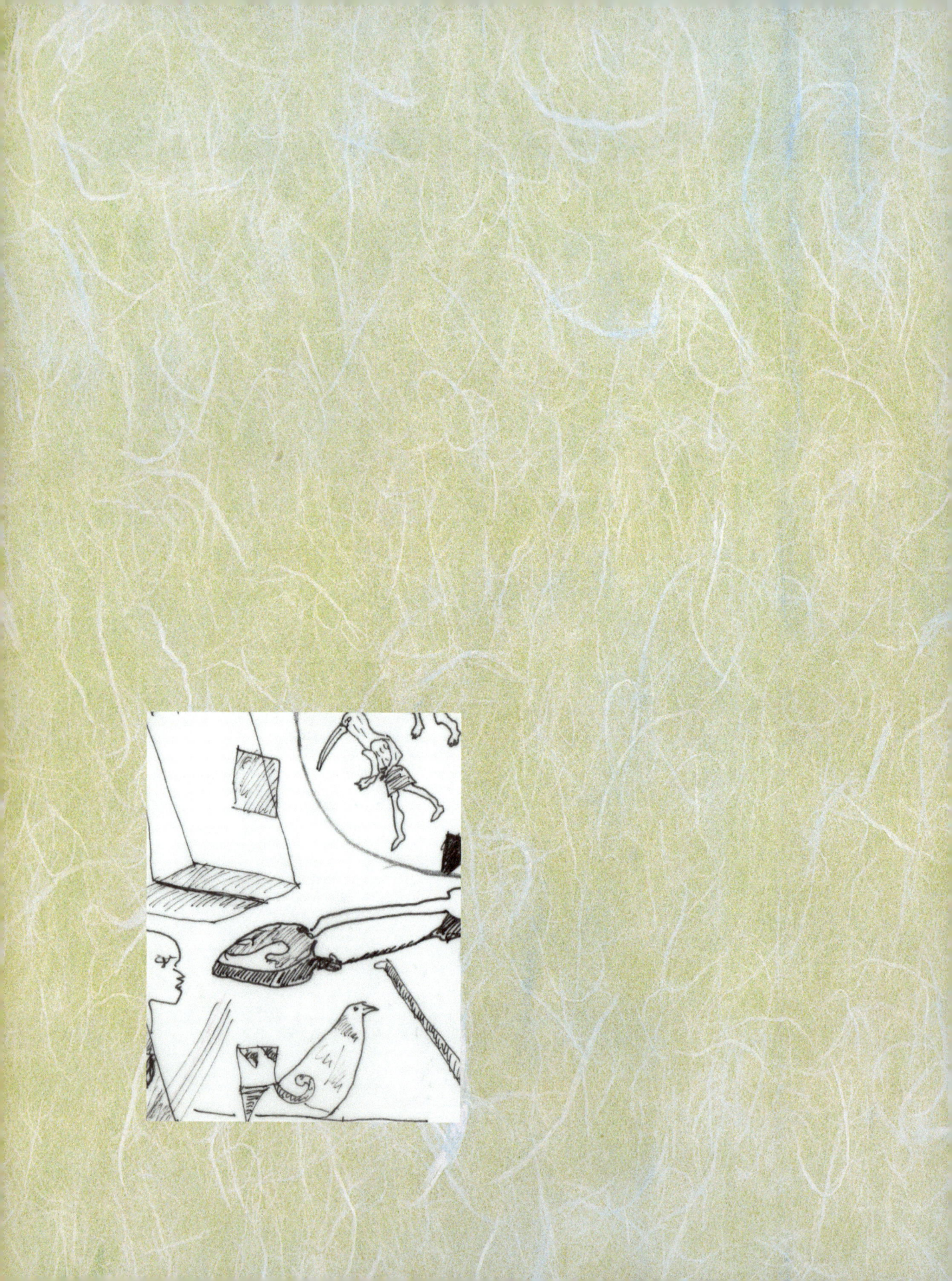

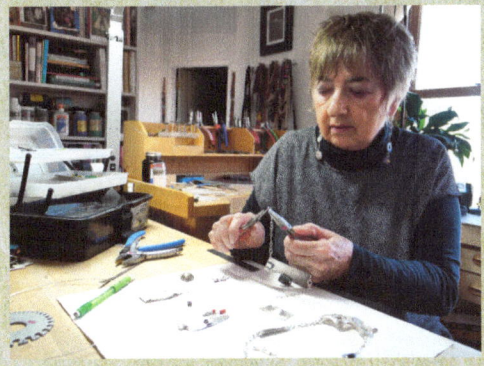

About the Artist/Author

Gloria Abella Ballen is an international award-winning author and visual artist. Her previous books *The Power of the Hebrew Alphabet,* The *New World Hagadah* (with Ilan Stavans) and *Garden of Eden* have each won best book awards, including other awards for design and production.

Abella Ballen has graduate degrees in art from SUNY-Buffalo as well as graduate studies in anthropology and Pre-Columbian art from the National School of Anthropology and History in Mexico City. She did special workshops in studio art and theory with Larry Rivers and John Cage.

She has exhibited in individual and group shows internationally (United States, United Kingdom, Israel, Italy, Mexico, Colombia, Japan) and has received awards from the UNESCO prize in painting to the Latin American Graphics Biennial, National Endowment for the Arts, the Pan American Graphics Portfolio Award, and the British Council among others.

Her art is in the collections of museums, corporations and private individuals internationally. She has been a visiting artist in England (University of Essex and the Camberwell School of Art), in China (University of Xinjiang), and in Israel (Mishkan Omanim in Herzliya). She has been a professor of art at universities in Puerto Rico, Colombia and the United States.

Abella Ballen currently lives in Santa Fe, New Mexico where she is the co-founder and organizer of the Santa Fe Distinguished Lecture Series and the Jewish Learning Channel. She can be seen commenting on her art on the Jewish Learning Channel.

Gaon Books
is the publishing arm of the
Institute for Tolerance Studies,
a 501-c-3 non-profit
organzation.

Gaon Books
www.gaonbooks.com

Creativity and Inspiration. Copyright 2022. Gloria Abella Ballen. All rights reserved. This publication is in copyright. Subject to statutory exception and to the provisions of relevant collective licensing agreements, no reproduction of any part may be made without the written permission of Gaon Books, except for brief quotations included in analytical articles, chapters, and reviews.

For permissions group pricing, and other information contact
Gaon Books, P.O. Box 23924, Santa Fe, NM 87502
or write to the editor at gaonbooks@gmail.com.

The paper used in this publication is acid free and meets all ANSI (American National Standards for Information Sciences) standards for archival quality paper.

Library of Congress Cataloging-in-Publication Data

Names: Ballen, Gloria Abella, author.
Title: Creativity and inspiration / Gloria Abella Ballen.
Description: [Santa Fe] : Gaon Books, [2022] | Summary: "This is a book about the creativity process for a visual artist. Gloria Abella Ballen gives an initial statement about her creative process and then the body of the book are pages from her notebooks where she writes about ideas, makes sketches, and shows the art work that has resulted from the writing and sketches. She says, "I start working and a dialogue begins between that which is appearing in the piece and myself. I work every day in the silence of my studio in the company of the plants and birds I see and hear through my windows. For this book I have taken pages from my sketchbooks from different times and places that show some of the sources of inspiration that have fed my silence in the studio and contributed to my art making.""-- Provided by publisher.
Identifiers: LCCN 2022000077 | ISBN 9781935604877 (paperback) | ISBN 9781935604891 (hardcover)
Subjects: LCSH: Ballen, Gloria Abella--Psychology. | Artists--United States--Psychology.
Classification: LCC N6537.B174 A35 2022 | DDC 709.73--dc23/eng/20220208
LC record available at https://lccn.loc.gov/2022000077